DARK OBSESSION

DARK OBSESSION

THE TRAGEDY AND THREAT OF
THE HOMOSEXUAL LIFESTYLE

TIMOTHY J. DAILEY

BROADMAN
&HOLMAN
PUBLISHERS

NASHVILLE, TENNESSEE

0-8054-2746-5

Published by Broadman & Holman Publishers,
Nashville, Tennessee

Dewey Decimal Classification: 306.76
Subject Heading: HOMOSEXUALITY \ SEXUAL BEHAVIOR

1 2 3 4 5 6 7 8 9 10 07 06 05 04 03

Contents

Introduction

SOMEWHERE I HAVE A photo of him—a picture of self-assured authority. Tall and impeccably dressed, a broad, handsome smile gracing his chiseled features. He is standing in a crowd outside Torrey-Gray Auditorium at my graduation from Moody Bible Institute in Chicago. In the years since that sunny June afternoon, I have often mused at how seemingly untroubled he was to be there—at the very mecca of conservative evangelicalism—among those who would have recoiled at his secret life.

It was a life that even I did not suspect—but perhaps that is too generous. Basking in the attention of a man who seemed to provide what my own father had difficulty giving me, I ignored the subtle messages, telling myself it could not possibly be true.

I was flattered that he had come, flying to Chicago on his corporate jet and making room for me in his busy schedule. The man I will call Alec Walker[1] was the vice president of a major U.S. corporation whose products could be found in any household. As we stood and talked among the clusters of robed graduates surrounded by family and friends, he pointed out—in his invariably perceptive way—that I was nervously chewing gum as I walked across the stage to receive my diploma. Alec had a charming ability to focus his attentions in a way that made people feel unique and valued.

1

As the crowds thinned and good-byes were said to classmates as our life paths diverged, I walked Alec through the tall crusader arches of Crowell Hall to catch a cab on LaSalle Avenue.

"Come with me!" he invited spontaneously, his eyes bright with anticipation. "We'll go up for the weekend to Camp Woodbrook!"

He caught me off guard—yet I couldn't help but get excited at the prospect. Alec owned some property with a private lake in Wisconsin. I felt honored that such an important person would clear his schedule to spend a few days with me. But at the same time, I was perplexed. I wasn't prepared for such a trip. Alec knew that my parents and siblings were waiting for me to return home with them. Although truly honored that Alec had come to my graduation, I thought he would understand that this was first and foremost a special time for them.

I awkwardly declined and watched Alec whisk off in his cab. It was almost like—no, it couldn't be. For a moment Alec seemed to be acting like someone in the throes of infatuation, trying to woo his would-be paramour to a romantic getaway. Alec—with his exalted position of responsibility, not to mention model wife and family? I turned back to my waiting family, putting the troubling thoughts out of my head.

But the nagging doubts did not go away. They gradually intensified until the issue of his homosexuality—and his desire to have a sexual relationship with me—were finally revealed one evening two years later during dinner at a swanky restaurant overlooking the Minneapolis skyline.

This is the story of unbounded potential and success tragically compromised by the dark, perverse sexual obsession that is homosexuality. It is about a lifestyle that all too often leads to duplicitous lives—for even "open" homosexuals feel compelled to conceal the full extent of their sordid sex lives lest their nongay friends and family be scandalized.

It is my hope that this book will strip away the false depiction of the gay lifestyle as presented by activists backed by the media and entertainment industry. "Coming out" is now defined as the exhilarating release from the repression and denial of one's true "sexual orientation." In truth, after coming out, the initial period of elation is typically followed by the sordid reality of the gay lifestyle, where one soon learns that love is equated with sex. When the sex wanes, the imagined love is nowhere to be found.

Many homosexuals—especially young men just entering the gay lifestyle—genuinely aspire to the romantic ideal. But they are invariably—and bitterly—disappointed, as the idealism of finding the perfect man to spend one's life with eventually degenerates into increasingly transient sexual relationships—culminating in a level of full-blown promiscuity that most heterosexuals would find scandalous.

The unavoidable descent into sexual immorality occurs because the gay lifestyle is by its very nature inimical to the kind of love and commitment upon which true, heterosexual romance and marriage are based. But by the time the truth has been learned, for many it is too late.

Homosexuality is for most people unfathomable: the thought of sexual relations between men and men—or women and women—is instinctively repulsive. Despite this, many people take a "live and let live" attitude toward homosexuals—an approach that is becoming increasingly difficult as gay activists relentlessly pursue their agenda.

I feel a deep sense of tragedy for those who are deceived by the activists' lies. Righteous anger is properly directed toward efforts to force the full acceptance—even celebration—of the gay lifestyle upon every aspect of society—in school, in marriage and family, in media and entertainment, even in the Christian church.

A word about terminology: As the reader will learn, Alec Walker described himself as "bisexual" (someone who engages in sexual relations with men and women). While this is true in that he had sexual relationships with men and his wife, rather than risk confusing the reader with terminology, I refer to his sexual proclivities as "homosexual." Webster's defines *homosexuality* as "sexual desire and behavior directed toward a person of one's own sex." Note that this definition does not preclude someone who *also* engages in heterosexual relations. Indeed, as we shall see, many homosexual men have at some time engaged in sexual relations with women.

This book is designed to shed light on the complex and mystifying phenomenon of homosexuality and to answer the question of whether homosexual behavior is compatible with the Christian faith. To answer that question we will examine the testimony of the Bible and Christian tradition regarding homosexual behavior.

We will examine the sordid nature of the gay lifestyle and ask, "Are people born gay?" along with the vital question, "Can homosexuals change?" As we seek to answer these questions, I hope this book will be of help to individuals struggling with the dark obsession that is homosexuality and to the concerned parents and pastors reaching out to them.

CHAPTER 1
"I'd Like You to Meet Alec"

WHY DO PEOPLE enter the homosexual lifestyle—is it because they were "born" that way or because of something that happened in their childhood? We will later examine the "nature versus nurture" argument raging among scientists in the field of human sexuality. One thing is clear: the causes of sexual attraction remain elusive because the sex drive itself is extraordinarily complex and goes to the very heart of our being.

A number of factors are believed to cause homosexual attraction, some of which have been listed in a report by the Catholic Medical Association:[1]

- Alienation from the father in early childhood because the father was perceived as hostile, distant, violent, or alcoholic.
- An overprotective mother who was needy and demanding or, conversely, emotionally unavailable.
- Parents who failed to instill same-sex identification (boys as males, girls as females).
- A lack of rough-and-tumble play or participation in team sports.
- Sexual abuse or rape.

- Social phobia or extreme shyness.
- Separation from parent through death, divorce, or temporal absence during critical developmental stages.
- Lack of hand/eye coordination and resultant teasing by peers (boys).

Homosexuals often make the claim, "As long as I can remember, I've always been gay." However, the fact that they may not be aware of what caused the same-sex attraction does not mean that it is "inborn." As the above list indicates, there are a wide variety of reasons why people might at an early age find themselves abnormally attracted to persons of the same sex.

Looking back, I can see that I was a candidate for entering the homosexual lifestyle, having exhibited some of the environmental factors known to cause homosexual feelings. These included a distant father, a devoted but strong-willed mother, and a feeling of not quite fitting in with my peers.

With nine children to raise, my parents were often not able to devote sufficient time and attention to each of us, and it soon became apparent that I was falling between the cracks. Even though the school-administered IQ tests indicated my high aptitude, I was barely passing each grade. Why? Because my overworked mother, instead of forcing us to do schoolwork, was too often content to have us go out to play after school in the tree-shaded yard and fields around our large old farmhouse. My early memories of my mother are of her cooking, washing dishes, and scrubbing floors. She loved her children dearly but had little time to spend with us individually.

My father was raised in a home on the poor side of town by emotionally distant parents. His half brothers and half sisters often treated him cruelly and let him know that, as his mother's illegitimate child, he was not fully a part of the family. He carried the emotional scars with him throughout his life. My father's earliest memory was of being traumatized in the night by his brother, who startled him awake with a gruesome-looking WWI gas mask. Though my father worked hard to provide for his family, he was not able to emotionally connect with his children. We knew that he loved us and would do what he could for us, but that love could only be expressed indirectly. I do not remember being hugged by my dad or verbally encouraged by him.

With no one at home to pay close attention to how I was doing, my homework went undone and I went to school day after day, dreading the consequences of my indolence. Despite my poor grades, my high-school teachers placed me in advanced courses because of my intelligence test results, hoping I would respond to the challenge. It didn't work. During my freshman year I failed all of my academic courses. Determined to avoid the shame of having flunked a grade, I repeated courses and attended summer school, somehow scraping by to graduate with my class.

For obvious reasons college didn't interest me. Why should I subject myself to more humiliating failure? However, there was one subject I was interested in studying. My mother was a strong Christian who had raised us children in the church. My travails during high school had caused me to turn to God, and I had developed a personal faith in Christ and a desire to learn about the Bible.

The school I chose to attend, Moody Bible Institute in downtown Chicago, afforded unlimited jobs that helped me pay for my schooling. While working downtown proved to be a learning experience in itself, once again my grades suffered. Long hours spent away from school at work also limited my social life—thus deepening my sense of isolation from classmates and peers.

In my junior year I acquired a roommate who would bring the most profound moral and spiritual challenge of my young life. Doug was a likeable fellow—outgoing and emotionally expressive. He came from a broken family and difficult upbringing. It was quite an accomplishment for him to be at Moody. One day as I walked into our dorm room, I was greeted by a tall, well-dressed man who had come to visit Doug. His name was Alec.

Doug met Alec while working as a parking lot attendant in downtown Minneapolis. He quickly stood out from among Doug's daily customers, and soon his warm greetings turned into conversation, which blossomed into friendship. Alec prodded his young friend to pursue his education, so Doug, having become a Christian, decided to apply to Moody Bible Institute. Later, when Doug was going through a difficult period, which led to dropping out of Moody, Alec motivated him to follow his dream of becoming a doctor. He wrote letters and made contacts that helped land Doug in medical school.

All this for a parking lot attendant. This was the Alec that would befriend me.

Getting to know Alec was a joy. It seemed he could carry on an informed conversation no matter what the topic. And when I was with Alec, his favorite topic always seemed to be me. He was uncannily observant, telling me things about myself that I never knew; insights about how I walked and talked, what I was good at and—most intriguingly for a young man unsure of his future—what I could excel at with a little encouragement.

It certainly wasn't that Alec's own life was so tedious that he preferred to lose himself in the lives of others. Far from it. I was pleasantly surprised by an invitation to visit him at his home in Minneapolis, and when I was finally initiated into Alec's world, I found it fascinating beyond anything I had ever seen.

CHAPTER 2
Alec's World

M Y EXCITEMENT AT the invitation to visit Alec was tempered by the fact that I had little money—and no car to drive to Minneapolis. Through my part-time employment at a car rental agency, I arranged to deliver a vehicle from a Chicago dealership to Minneapolis. When I arrived at the dealership, however, I was dismayed at the aged pickup truck that would be my transportation. What the dealership in Minneapolis intended to do with such a wreck I will never know. Besides being an eyesore, the major flaw of the vehicle was that it stopped dead every time I took my foot off the gas pedal. Undeterred, I set off for Minneapolis with just enough pocket money for gas.

The trip was relatively uneventful until, passing through the farmlands of northern Wisconsin, the truck ominously began to lose strength. The rearview mirror revealed a thick cloud of black smoke trailing behind the truck. Alarmed, I barely managed to make it to the next exit, where the overheated pickup rolled to a stop and refused to budge.

Miraculously, there in the midst of miles of cornfields stood an automobile garage. I neglected to inform the mechanic that I had no money to pay for the new water pump until the work was completed, and then convinced him to give me a bill, which I later presented to the dealership. I have always hoped they paid it.

It was rush hour as I drove through downtown Minneapolis. The truck stalled at every stoplight until I finally arrived at the very parking lot where my roommate Doug had met Alec. I was soon ushered into Alec's glamorous life as a top executive of a major corporation in the heart of thriving Minneapolis.

I stepped out of the elevator onto the plush executive floor of the company's headquarters. Alec's secretary ushered me into a starkly modern office, gleaming of chrome and steel. It suited him perfectly. He emerged behind a massive mahogany desk and greeted me effusively.

Alec was not one to be constrained in an office for long. Eager to show me around, he took me through the skyways connecting the downtown stores and offices, offering trivia about the city as we walked. Alec greeted numerous friends and acquaintances as we made our way through the bustling, shop-lined walkways. It seemed like he knew everyone in town. At one point a handsome man in a business suit swept toward us and exchanged a warm greeting with Alec as we passed. Alec turned and whispered to me, "He's gay!" Startled, I looked back to see the man looking back over his shoulder amusedly at us, as if thinking, *Look at Alec's new toy!* Was Alec checking my reaction? If so, my naive mind failed to compute what had just taken place.

As Alec's workday came to a close, instead of heading directly home as I expected, he took me to a bar downtown, a noisy, bawdy establishment with bowls of peanuts on the tables and discarded shells on the floor. It was here that I had my first inkling that something was amiss. As I sipped on a soft drink, wondering what we were doing there, Alec ordered a stiff drink, quickly followed by another and yet another. Coming from a home with a strict teetotaling mother, I was taken aback by how Alec effortlessly knocked back double martinis. As sheltered from the evils of the world as I was, I at least realized one thing: somehow, somewhere, something was wrong.

That evening Alec took me to his home where I met his wife, Rachel—a friendly, down-to-earth complement to her magnetic husband. I also met their four children: Carlos, Juanita, Drew, and Marie. Alec and Rachel had one of those rare marriages between two gifted and sociable individuals who seem to complete each other perfectly. They enjoyed a storybook marriage of adventure and personal sacrifice combined with exemplary public service. As a young couple Alec and Rachel left budding, promising careers to serve in the Peace Corps, where they lived in the impoverished seaside town of Manta, Ecuador, helping to establish local sanitation, schools, and industry. When they returned to the States they adopted and brought with them four-year-old Carlos along with his three-year-old sister Juanita. Later, along with their biological son, Drew, the Walkers would adopt still another child, Marie, in Minnesota.

The Walkers lived in a lovely home on the shores of beautiful Lake Excelsior outside Minneapolis. The house wasn't extravagant: Alec and Rachel were the antithesis of pretention. He had engaged a handsome young architect to remodel the house and surround it with spacious patios and balconies. As Alec introduced me to the architect, praising his work on the remodeling project, I admired his gift of bringing out the best in people.

Showing me around his home, Alec regaled me with stories of politicians and actors he knew. Autographed photos of his friend, former vice president Hubert Humphrey, and other notables adorned the walls of the Walker home.

Later, as I sat alone in the dining room looking through some family photos, Alec came up behind me. He put his hands on my shoulders, leaned over, and kissed me on the back of my neck. Looking back I am amazed and embarrassed that I did not recognize the sexual signal. While such actions made me uncomfortable, in my ignorance I attributed them to Alec's open, warm, and responsive personality.

Although I was sitting in the dining room, I was surprised to learn that there would be no dinner together with the family. Rachel and the children were off somewhere, and Alec and I were alone. The fact that no one else was around made it possible for him to openly make a move on me.

During another visit to the Walker home, once again Alec "arranged" to be alone with me in the house. I had arranged to meet a fellow Moody student who lived in next-door St. Paul and go out to see a movie together. We weren't dating, but when I told Alec of my plans for the evening he had an odd reaction. He seemed miffed, put off, *jealous!* I shook off his inexplicable response and went on my way.

When I returned later that evening, the house was dark except for the stairway light, as if to invite me upstairs. I felt distinctly uncomfortable. I wished Rachel was around, but she and the children were gone, likely to Woodbrook Lake in Wisconsin. It seemed that Alec had the magical ability to make the rest of the family disappear in order to set up moments such as these.

Good manners left me little choice but to bid good night to my host lest I appear unfriendly. So I trudged upstairs, reluctant to intrude on the Walkers's private living space. I cautiously knocked on the bedroom door. Alec beckoned me in, and I entered to see him stretched out languidly—and expectantly—on their big bed in his sexy, bright-colored briefs. Thoroughly embarrassed, I made some small talk while averting my gaze.

At my first opportunity I hastily excused myself. Alec's disappointment and frustration was obvious as I said good night and managed to extricate myself from the room. My "date" had likely disrupted whatever designs he had for the evening.

As I look back on my visits to the Walkers's home, I have no memory of sharing a meal with the family or sitting around talking with Alec, Rachel, and the children in the living room. My recollections are invariably of an empty house with almost a sense of loneliness. How could this be, given Alec and Rachel's active, outgoing lives where there was seemingly not a boring moment?

The reason is that, though unspoken and perhaps unrealized by all, I was a destructive intruder, and by my very presence I threatened the Walker family and stole precious time from their life together. Of course, being unaware of (or at least unable to face up to) Alec's motives, I was an unwitting participant in his designs.

I'll never forget a perceptive remark about the effects of sexual immorality on families: When a husband/father is involved in adultery, the clandestine relationship sucks emotional energy out of the home—*and the wife and children intuitively feel the loss.*

I am certain that Alec did not directly intend to harm his family, but his actions devoted his emotional energy to me rather than those who needed and deserved his attention. If his intentions had been morally upright, I would have been naturally integrated into the Walker family as a friend of Alec's—and been therefore accepted by Rachel and the children. I would have enjoyed being together with Alec and his family—yet those times never seemed to happen.

As it was, Alec craftily arranged for his family to be gone from the house so that he could "entertain" me without interruption. And I was by no means the only one. I gradually realized that Alec's young male "friends" occupied a good share of his time and energy.

Later Alec took me out for a sail on Lake Excelsior. As we glided across the deep green water, I asked about a picturesque restaurant across the lake. Alec promptly said he would take me there. He never did, but no matter, with Alec every day brought exciting new possibilities. I now realize I enjoyed a pampered existence during the time spent with him, receiving interest and attention I rarely, if ever, found growing up in a big family of modest income.

That evening in his kitchen, Alec described the food products his company sold, making me eager to try them. He had the ability to relate interesting facts and information about everything around him, making the most mundane subject appealing. He promised to bake one of the products in the morning but, as usual, we were up and off without further ado. Alec had already moved onto the next challenge and curiosity in his fascinating life.

In odd ways, Alec was unaffected by the trappings of luxury. When we commuted to downtown Minneapolis, he did not drive an expensive sedan. We rode in a used Volkswagen that Alec had bought from a friend. He would hang his leg out the window in the summer heat because the car lacked air conditioning.

I appreciated that the Walkers were not materialistic. In fact they gave every indication of being the model American family active in civic affairs, the arts, and their church. They were kind and generous to a fault. But I would soon discern that underneath the idealistic surface swirled troubling undercurrents.

A Charmed, Troubled Life

Alec George Walker was born in 1933, in Newton, Massachusetts, a pleasant town of tree-lined streets and Gothic churches. Alec remembered his father, a plumber, as a man who liked music, played a harmonica, and sang. His mother, Dorothy, was a quiet, unassuming woman who placed few constraints upon her adventurous son. As early as age eight, Alec was allowed to be gone all day from home playing at the beach. His older sister, Marjorie, remembers the young Alec as a creative and imaginative child who raised mice in the bathtub and liked to rearrange the furniture in the house.

Alec's childhood memories would not all be idyllic. Storm clouds were brewing in the Walker household even as war broke out in Europe. When Alec was nine years old, his father joined the army and went off to fight in World War II. During the war

Dorothy went to work in a shoe factory. When Alec Sr.'s tour of duty ended, the fighting did not stop but continued in their home. Dorothy worked long hours at the factory, and as her marriage to Alec Sr. disintegrated into constant quarreling, Alec, then twelve, and his younger brother went to live with relatives in nearby Merrimac.

Alec Sr. and Dorothy eventually divorced. Shortly afterward Dorothy married a man she had met at the factory while Alec Sr. was overseas. Alec had intermittent contact with his father until, at age fifty-three, Alec Sr. died of a heart attack while bowling after having all his teeth pulled.

Alec gave every indication of thriving in Merrimac. He was a very good student in high school; he sang in school musical productions, including a solo role in the Gilbert and Sullivan operettas. He excelled at sports, especially basketball. Alec was also active in the local Methodist church. He sang in the choir and was president of the youth group. After school he worked as the church janitor.

Following high school Alec attended the University of Wisconsin in Madison. There he continued his involvement in the church. His social life revolved around the Wesley Foundation Student Center for Methodist students. He sang in the student choir and joined in the many activities of the student center. As a zealous Methodist he carried a Bible around with him to all his classes.

It was while singing in the Wesley Foundation choir that Alec met his future wife, Rachel. Alec, two years older and a junior at the university, took note of the stately freshman from northern Minnesota. Rachel remembers that she and Alec never went on formal "dates" together. Alec was not interested in conventions, which was one of the many unique qualities that attracted Rachel to him. Instead, they got to know each other while participating in group activities like campouts and retreats organized by the Wesley Foundation.

The budding romance between Alec and Rachel was periodically interrupted when Alec was forced to drop out of school to earn money. Having no financial support from his family, he had to work his way through college. Rachel remembers how Alec would go back east to work in a hospital on Long Island. While there he would live at home with his mother and stepfather.

Rachel graduated from the university, taught school for a year, and announced that she was joining the Methodist missionary service to serve in Africa as a teacher. Alec, working on the East Coast, heard the news and made a beeline back to Madison. He proposed to Rachel, telling her, "They don't need you in Africa as much as I need you here. Let's get married and then we can go to Africa together!"

Having had a crush on Alec for years, Rachel was delighted and said yes immediately. As for why she did not need time to think it over, she said, "I was attracted to Alec because of his creativity, his sense of humor, his kind ways, his talent, and his enthusiasm for life. He was extremely unusual for the times—always with fresh ideas, never in a rut. He didn't behave in the ordinary ways of the other guys I dated. He was the one for me!"

So in 1958, without ever having a real date, Rachel and Alec decided to marry. They chose Pine Lake Camp, a Methodist retreat center, for the wedding ceremony, with Rachel's father, Rev. John Parker, officiating.

Needless to say, Rachel canceled her plans to go to Africa. Yet the idealism of service to one's fellowman—of not following the stereotypical American goals of a business career and life in the suburbs—continued to strike a deep chord in both Alec and Rachel. The newlyweds began looking for opportunities to serve together overseas.

Two years later, in 1960, during his impromptu speech at the University of Michigan, presidential candidate John F. Kennedy challenged Americans to give two years of their lives to help people in the developing world. The following year the Peace Corps was born.

As they awaited opportunities for service, the Walkers settled into married life in Geneva, Illinois, where Alec worked as a sales engineer and Rachel taught school. In the Walkers's biographical account of their Peace Corps work in a small seaside village in Ecuador, Alec describes those active days: "We had a wonderful life. Besides our jobs, we had many friends. We lived full, twenty-four-hour days. Our hobbies included canoeing, camping, singing, painting, bicycling, and little-theater work. We were close to our church, helped with its youth group, and took part in reading and discussion groups."

The Walkers's book is filled with the 1960s idealism that motivated young people to aspire to change the world. In it Rachel quotes a motivational speaker of the day who captured the aspirations of many in their generation: "Dedicate some of your life to others. Your dedication will not be a sacrifice. It will be an exhilarating experience because it is an intense effort applied toward a meaningful end. My wish is that you will utilize yourself as a force of unity in the fragile peace of today. And that you will know the happiness that comes of serving others who have nothing."

The Walkers enthusiastically applied for the Peace Corps and even wrote to President Kennedy about their appreciation for the program. "Dear Mr. President," Rachel wrote, "There finally has come about an organized effort that offers us, as a couple, an opportunity to fulfill an earnest and sincere desire to serve less fortunate people abroad." In the letter she alludes to the fact that, at age twenty-six, Alec had already shown potential for what would later be a meteoric rise in the business world: "We offer ourselves to the Peace Corps," she wrote, "not because we are at loose ends in our lives or between jobs. In three years, Alec's job responsibility and salary have doubled."

Newlyweds Abroad

After waiting a year and almost giving up hope, Alec and Rachel were finally accepted and spent three months of intensive training in Puerto Rico, during which 40 percent of the group dropped out. Alec and Rachel graduated and were assigned to Manta, Ecuador.

Leaving the comforts of home behind, the Walkers were in for a rude surprise when they saw their new residence in a poverty-stricken seaside neighborhood: "The place was dark and crowded, full of boxes, old furniture, pelts, and scrap metal, and permeated with the overwhelming odor of dead rats. It was one big room, with one corner partially walled off. There was no electricity, no water system, no kitchen, no toilet, and no windows except for the jail bars."

After a thorough housecleaning and refitting of the apartment with homemade furniture, curtains, and a jury-rigged kitchen, Alec and Rachel plunged into organizing community action projects to assist the dirt-poor residents of the neighborhood. After hearing that the annual onslaught of bubonic plague had arrived, Alec mobilized the men to construct trash containers and clear the refuse from the streets that was feeding the disease-carrying rats.

Believing that education and training were keys to the Ecuadorians' future, Alec taught carpentry and automobile repair to the young men of the neighborhood, while Rachel taught hygiene, home improvement, and swimming classes. Seeing that the local school had no facilities to cook lunch for the students, Alec and Rachel planned and supervised the building of a kitchen where hot meals could be prepared, providing nutritious meals for the students, many of whom suffered from malnutrition.

Latin culture emphasizes relationships and hospitality, and the Walkers spent many happy hours visiting their neighbors and hosting friends who would drop by unannounced throughout the day. Alec and Rachel served as makeshift nurses, teachers, builders, artisans, and counselors for the seaside neighborhood. The community welcomed the young American couple into their lives and soon became attached to them. Judging from the Walkers's account of their life in Manta, the feeling was unreservedly mutual.

Decades later, Rachel looked back upon their time in Ecuador: "It was a wonderful experience. We loved speaking Spanish and working with the humblest people. At the end we adopted two little children from our barrio, and that has changed our lives. They are now forty-one and forty-two years old, parents of their own children and outstanding citizens of the U.S.A. Having Carlos and Juanita and being a part of the lives of their children has been the most rewarding experience of my life."

Writing almost forty years earlier, a youthful Alec echoes his wife's joy at their married life together in Ecuador:

> We personally had never experienced anything as satisfying and fulfilling for us as a couple as our two years in the Peace Corps. I often looked at Rachel, quietly explaining to the mother of a sick infant how to make baby food or mixing a glass of powdered milk for Carlos, and wondered if I would have ever had the courage to come down here alone. Having each other to lean on for support in moments of crisis (like the plague epidemic) or just having each other to share a good meal of fried tuna or a beautiful sunset were memorable rewards of married life in the Peace Corps.

In 1964, at the end of their service in Ecuador with the Peace Corps, Alec and an expecting Rachel returned to the United States, bringing with them Carlos and Juanita from Manta. Alec had no job, and they had no money or place to stay. Rachel's parents, John and Alma Parker, who lived in the Twin Cities, invited the budding young family to stay with them. Alec,

Rachel, and their two adopted children moved into the Parkers's spacious parsonage.

During the year they were there, Rachel gave birth to a boy, Drew. Some years later the Walkers also adopted an eighteen-month-old girl, Marie, who was of mixed black and Puerto Rican racial background.

This willingness to open their home and extend their love and compassion to the less fortunate was characteristic of Alec and Rachel. I often wondered how many of my "theologically correct" fellow evangelical Christians—including myself—demonstrated a similar love and concern for others as commanded in the New Testament.

In 1965 Alec began his dazzling career in the business world. He was offered a position at a department store in downtown Minneapolis, where he eventually was promoted to vice president of Public Affairs. In 1970 he assumed the position of vice president of Corporate Communications and officer of the company he was working for when I met him. He also headed a philanthropic foundation and found time to be a part-time professor in the business school of a local university.

When I met him, Alec was approaching the pinnacle of his success. I remember him relating with genuine surprise how his salary doubled and doubled again as he assumed increasing responsibility and the accompanying prestige in the business world.

But all was not well in Camelot. I sensed that at the end of one of my visits to Excelsior. Alec had departed earlier for the city. Rachel came out to see me off as I was taking my luggage out to the used yellow Volkswagen bug that I had managed to purchase. As I stood in the garage with my bags she unburdened herself cryptically without revealing specifics. I listened politely, feeling somehow uneasy. How could a young man like me possibly relate to the accomplished wife of someone like Alec?

I got the distinct impression that Rachel wanted to reach a deeper level of communication. Finally she let me go, saying, "Thanks for being my confidant." *Confidant?* Wasn't Alec her confidant? The thought raced through my mind that I was speaking to a woman hungry to share her feelings—or perhaps to have her fears assuaged. I later wondered if Rachel suspected something untoward in Alec's and my relationship and was attempting to broach the subject with me that morning.

Something was wrong with this idyllic picture of a family in a charming house on a picturesque lake. Much later I would realize that I was seeing what appeared to be the perfect love story being smashed to bits on the shores of Lake Excelsior. I remembered photos of a youthful, smiling, tanned Alec and Rachel in Ecuador, full of purpose, vitality, and hope for the future. What crushed those dreams? I would not have long to wait for the answer.

CHAPTER 3

"It's Time We Made a Decision about Our Relationship"

A FEW MONTHS LATER, the time punctuated by telephone calls from Alec with yet another invitation to visit, I again found myself in Minneapolis. As usual, he showered attention on me, treating me like a pampered prince. On my last evening in town, he took me to an expensive restaurant with a panoramic view of downtown Minneapolis. But as I sat down I had a vague uneasiness about Alec's designs for the evening. It was almost—no, surely not—as if I were being courted.

My forebodings were confirmed as I chiseled away a huge portion of prime rib. After the usual pleasant conversation, Alec broached the subject: "I thought it was time we decided where our relationship was going."

Where our relationship was going? I immediately had a sinking feeling. All the questions and red flags I was desperately hoping were not true were confirmed. I did not want our relationship to "go anywhere." I was perfectly content to continue bathing in the glow of Alec's focused attention. I had almost convinced myself that Alec found me endlessly interesting because of who I was—not for reasons I dared not contemplate. I did not want to confront the harsh reality that now loomed. But the bill for Alec's solicitation was about to be delivered, and payment was expected in full.

I was reluctantly drawn into what turned out to be a grueling spiritual confrontation. The dinner and surroundings faded as the stage cleared for—what was for Alec, at least—a long-awaited encounter. For the rest of the evening I, like a novice swordsman, tried to parry the skillful attacks of a master fencer as we engaged in verbal sparring that taxed my abilities.

The prize was nothing less than my sexuality. Would I this very evening be initiated into homosexuality, or would I preserve my chastity and what I had been taught about immoral sexual behavior? The ramifications of each possible outcome were far-reaching: this evening literally contained the potential for determining the very course of my life.

Yet as the battle was joined, I was surprised to discover reserves of inner strength I did not know existed. I would later realize that the scriptural promise was being fulfilled on my behalf: "Do not worry beforehand about what to say. Just say whatever is given you at the time, for it is not you speaking, but the Holy Spirit" (Mark 13:11 NIV).

Energized by the unseen power within me, I took the initiative, questioning Alec about what he considered to be his "sexual orientation." He played mind games with me, throwing me for a loop by denying that he was homosexual. Yet he confirmed that he wasn't heterosexual. I was stumped. Then, with a glint in his eye, he revealed the answer: he was bisexual.

This exchange with Alec was my introduction to the fluid concept of sexual orientation. I would later learn that homosexual activists use this term to justify their sexual proclivities, insisting that those tendencies are inborn and thus unchangeable. The term has also become a powerful argument for extending special rights and privileges for homosexuals. However, unlike the category of race, homosexuality is not an immutable characteristic.

We cannot change our racial heritage, but—as we shall see—we can alter our sexual behavior.

The discussion in the restaurant turned to how Alec became involved in homosexuality. He described one of his early homosexual encounters. I do not know why he opened up to me: it may have been a cathartic release for him to confess his immoral experiences to someone. Or he may have shared his sexual encounters in the expectation that they would awaken what he hoped were similar urges within me.

"My friend and I were camping," he explained. "We shared a small cabin—just a table, a couple of chairs, and bunk beds. It was late—we'd been sitting and talking for quite awhile—about nothing in particular. The time came to go to bed. We turned out the lights. I climbed into my bunk."

He paused for effect. "Instead of climbing up to his own bunk, he climbed into bed with me." Alec watched my reaction. I was having trouble digesting all this. I found it quite incredible and asked the first question that came to mind in the vain hope that Alec was describing a one-time experience.

"Have there been others?" I asked, not wanting to face up to the growing possibility that Alec was engaged in a hidden life of homosexual promiscuity.

"Yes!" hissed Alec, as if I'd wrung a confession from him and should have known there were others—many others.

As Alec described his "bisexuality," he assured me that he and Rachel had a great sex life together. Even though I knew little about homosexuality, I wondered if he was exposing his wife to sexually transmitted diseases from his sexual contacts. As we shall see in a later chapter, STDs are rampant in the gay community.

Nature called and I excused myself. As I did, Alec made a crude remark about my going to the washroom. He may have been trying to get me to let down my guard and participate in lubricious "sex talk." Having only seen Alec's polite, well-mannered side, I was surprised to hear him talking like that, and the comment made me realize how sexualized his thinking was. Realizing the goal of Alec's solicitous interest and concern for me made me wonder how many countless young men have been seduced into the homosexual lifestyle by men who feigned genuine love for them.

Upon returning to our table, I saw the first crack in Alec's confident demeanor when I asked him if Rachel knew of his sexual relationships with men. He would only say, "She knows that I have never been with another woman." Coming from Alec, this was no mean accomplishment. I remember his report of women constantly throwing themselves at him, not caring that he was married.

The fact that he resisted the advances of other women served, for Alec, as justification for his double life. After all, in one respect he was indeed "faithful." Like many people, Alec preferred to balance his sin against what he considered to be the good he accomplished. As if dismissing his homosexual contacts as inconsequential, he assured me: "This is just 1 percent of my life. The other 99 percent is what matters. That will be my legacy."

I had heard similar logic used by men involved in extramarital affairs. In one case a man worked hard every year preparing his department budget—a difficult job that he dreaded. When the long process was finally completed, he would reward himself by hiring a homosexual prostitute. Just once a year—the rest of the time he was "faithful" to his wife.

Another man, a professor, attends an academic conference every year. And each year he "treats" himself to a prostitute. The kids receive their presents at Christmas; he gets his at the conference. Then the professor goes home to his wife and doesn't stray the remainder of the year.

I doubt if the wives of either of these men would buy the "99 percent faithful" argument—just as I frankly doubted that Rachel would accept such a self-serving perversion of the concept of marital faithfulness.

I also doubted Alec's contention that his extramarital sexual behavior occupied such a small fraction of his time and energy. Like the proverbial camel that is permitted to stick its nose into the tent—and soon occupies the tent—sexual obsessions tend to take over a person's life. Those in the throes of a passionate adulterous affair are consumed by it, desiring to be with their paramour at all costs, heedless of their deprived spouse.

I thought about how to respond to Alec's "1 percent" remark. "You know, Alec," I replied, "all it takes is one moment of passion to change our lives forever.

"Come to think of it," I continued, "a lot of murderers would love to be let off the hook by appealing to the '99 percent' argument. But no self-respecting judge would let them walk. That's because a lifetime of 'good' does not give us immunity from the consequences of our wrong actions."

Alec was proving to be a skillful and elusive opponent. No sooner had one line of reasoning failed than he tried another. This time he attempted a more personal tactic—one designed to circumvent my sexual inhibitions.

"I have a suggestion," he said innocently. "Why don't we just lie together in bed?" He added, "We don't have to 'do' anything. What's wrong with that?"

I was appalled at this suggestion—and by the fact that Alec apparently thought it had a chance of success. I also gained sudden insight into Alec's formidable seductive charms. On how many other occasions had a similar ruse worked? How many young men had he maneuvered into bed—men who didn't plan on becoming sexually involved with him but could not stand against the "harmless" proposal of simply sharing the same bed?

But there was no way I would consider such a thing—even if I couldn't think of a response to his offer. I realized he was asking me to lead myself into temptation to prove I was strong enough to resist. At this point my rudimentary knowledge about rational argumentation (provided by a long-standing interest in Christian apologetics) kicked in.

"You probably know that Rush Street—the 'entertainment capital of the Midwest'—is a few blocks from Moody Bible Institute," I said. "You can walk down Rush and participate in just about any kind of vice imaginable. The outlines of dancing girls are reflected through the windows of strip joints. Drug dealers and prostitutes—male and female—ply their trades on the street. Yet its location next to the upscale Magnificent Mile of Lake Shore Drive gives it a touristy legitimacy it doesn't deserve. In fact, groups of Moody students go over for the great pizza at Gino's restaurant.

"But pizza is one thing; sexual titillation is another. I've spent many a lonely evening in my room on the nineteenth floor of Culbertson Hall overlooking the night life of Rush Street in the distance. And quite honestly, I've been tempted to walk over there. Sometimes it seems like the devil is saying to me, 'Go ahead, just do it! No one will know you were ever there. Go and have a look around; gaze at the outlines of the girls projected on the smoky glass. It can't hurt to just look!'

"But by God's grace I've never done it. I realize that if I put myself in the place of temptation, I will soon be at the mercy of powerful drives and uncontrollable circumstances. And that is exactly the strategy of the Evil One. But as long as I don't take that first step, I'm safe. So in those times of temptation I either stay put in my room or find some wholesome activity."

Proverbs 5:1–9—a passage that speaks to adultery and sexual temptation—came to mind:

> My son, pay attention to my wisdom,
>   listen well to my words of insight,
> that you may maintain discretion
>   and your lips may preserve knowledge.
> For the lips of an adulteress drip honey,
>   and her speech is smoother than oil;

but in the end she is bitter as gall,
    sharp as a double-edged sword.
Her feet go down to death;
    her steps lead straight to the grave.
She gives no thought to the way of life;
    her paths are crooked, but she knows it not.

Now then, my sons, listen to me;
    do not turn aside from what I say.
Keep to a path far from her,
    do not go near the door of her house,
lest you give your best strength to others
    and your years to one who is cruel. (NIV)

These verses warn of the seductive power of the temptress—and the tempter—whose lips "drip honey" and whose "speech is smoother than oil." How much silken speech has been employed in the service of deceitful causes! How many have entered the home—let alone the bedroom—of the adulteress in a foolish and futile attempt to persuade her of the evil of her ways! By that point too much vital territory has been conceded, and the battle is all but lost.

The way to victory over temptation is to resist while it is still possible to stand your ground—before the first step is taken. Thus the admonition: "Keep to a path far from her, do not go near the door of her house."

The emphasis here is not on being strong enough to withstand temptation; the issue is avoiding temptation from the outset. We must be so determined to fight temptation that we refuse to take the first seemingly innocuous baby steps in the direction of moral failure. Tragically, untold numbers of men—and women—have succumbed to temptation by failing to observe this simple yet effective rule.

The admonition of Proverbs reminds me of a Christian businessman who went on a business trip far from home. After a long day of meetings, he went to the hotel dining room and sat down to eat dinner. During the course of his meal he happened to strike up a conversation with a woman at a nearby table. The man discovered that they shared similar interests. Moreover, he found her sense of humor exhilarating.

The two of them hit it off so well that the man invited her to share his table, where they enjoyed stimulating conversation late into the evening. Then the woman invited the man up to her room for a drink. Despite being a teetotaler, he accepted, with the (at that point) inevitable immoral result.

Afterward, it was difficult for him to accept that he had actually committed adultery. On that fateful evening he felt he was observing someone else's infidelity with a detached sense of incredulity. Now he was faced with the awful dilemma of either confessing his adultery to his wife or burying the guilt and shame and pretending nothing happened. The man realized, to his unending regret that, like Esau, he "for one morsel of meat sold his birthright" (Heb. 12:16 KJV).

Where did this Christian man go wrong? To find the answer let's roll back the tape of that evening and note that he chose to sit next to an attractive woman. Why did he not obey the wisdom of Proverbs and choose a table far from possible temptation? And if he had no choice regarding his seating, why did he not keep to himself rather than engaging the woman in conversation?

Far from the restraints of home, the man was already in a vulnerable situation. By the time he struck up a conversation, which turned into "harmless" flirting, the snowball of lust and immorality was already hurtling toward the precipice.

Often we do not resist *before* the very first step because we actually desire to entertain temptation—at least for a season. We assure ourselves that we can always resist later. But the vital choice is made in that nascent stage, not when full-blown temptation presents itself. And then when we succumb, we excuse the sin by secretly assuring ourselves that it really was unavoidable—that under the circumstances, anyone else would have done the same. So we assuage our guilty conscience.

Back at the restaurant, Alec had one more argument to try on me, framing my moral objection to homosexuality in terms of a narrow-minded refusal to "love" men in the same way as women: "Do you really want to limit who you love by excluding half the human race?"

To Alec's way of thinking, by closing myself off to the possibility of homosexual relationships, I was losing out on a whole world of "loving possibilities." This one was easy.

"Alec," I replied, "I intend to exclude 'loving' the *entire* human race—except for my wife."

I was becoming a little piqued. Alec was not asking me to consider faithful, monogamous homosexual "love" (not that such a thing exists or that it would have changed my answer). He was expecting me to become his lover *du jour.* He wanted me to fulfill his sexual fantasies for as long as he remained infatuated with me.

Alec wanted only to initiate me into the homosexual lifestyle, with scant attention paid to the long-term consequences for my life. Entering the gay lifestyle as a young man would surely lead down the path of homosexual promiscuity—a path loaded with sexual identity confusion and sexually transmitted diseases that could result in a life cut short.

I do not imagine Alec would have consciously wished any of these negative consequences upon anyone. Beginning with his sacrificial service in the Peace Corps and continuing to the time I knew him, Alec devoted considerable efforts to helping people. However, at that moment Alec was gripped by the anticipated fulfillment of his lusts, which took precedence over wisdom about future consequences.

Amazingly, the tables were turning. The evening, which for Alec had begun so promisingly with the prospect of a long-awaited sexual conquest, was now developing quite differently than he had expected. As his early confidence evaporated, he grew strangely distant and morose.

Gone was the self-assured raconteur, confident of his next conquest. A dark, brooding side was emerging—a side few if any had had the opportunity to observe. An aura of hopelessness and utter pessimism began to envelop him. "Eventually Rachel will leave me," he said. "Someday I'll be alone." I didn't know how to respond; after seeing his secret life of adultery with other men, I wouldn't have been surprised if she did leave him.

The evening petered out. Alec seemed genuinely hurt by my declining his advances. We drove home in silence.

That evening as I went downstairs to the bunk bed in the rec room, for the first time in the Walkers's house, I was anxious. With Rachel and the children gone, I was afraid Alec would come down to my bed. As I tossed and turned, reliving the shocking evening, I heard footsteps descending the stairs. I prayed silently that Alec would not bother me—and to his credit, he didn't. After retrieving some clothes from the laundry room, he went back upstairs.

The next morning I drove with Alec to Camp Woodbrook, the Walkers's vacation retreat in northern Wisconsin. As tension was still high, I was glad we weren't alone. Doug, my former roommate, was invited. We sat together in the back seat. Doug was about to begin his studies at the university. I encouraged him not to neglect his spiritual life and to seek Christian fellowship.

As I spoke with Doug I saw Alec glaring at me in the rearview mirror, evidently livid at my sexual rejection of him from the previous night. My attempt to spiritually motivate Doug brought Alec's anger to the fore, and he directed a dismissive barb at me.

My concern was now for Doug. Knowing what I now did regarding Alec's homosexuality, I suddenly feared for my former roommate. When we arrived at Camp Woodbrook I tried to warn Doug about Alec. It was a difficult conversation because I had told Alec the night before that I would keep our conversation private, so I did not feel at liberty to share everything with Doug. All I could do was obliquely caution him to avoid compromising situations with Alec. I hoped Doug would catch on, but his response worried me. I also remembered him confiding to me earlier that Alec liked to take him swimming and to wrestle with him in the water. I eventually lost contact with Doug and can only hope that there was no impropriety in his relationship with Alec.

That evening I retired early. Alec woke me up at the crack of dawn to take me to the airport for my flight home. "You should have stayed up last night," he chided me. "We went skinny-dipping in the lake. And Rachel and Doug argued theology until the wee hours of the morning!"

Alec was amused. I tried to picture the conversation: Doug, with his evangelical fervor contending for the truthfulness of the Bible and the uniqueness of Jesus as Savior and God, and Rachel, with her liberal Protestant leanings, patiently trying to poke holes in his arguments.

As I was still a penniless student now attending the University of Wisconsin, Alec paid for my ticket home. Gone was the magic, the devoted attention, the palpable excitement at being together. As I walked across the tarmac to the airplane, he waved me off for what would be the last time. It would be many years before I learned the rest of Alec's story.

CHAPTER 4

The Bible and Homosexuality

I OFTEN WONDERED IF, on that last cool evening in the pristine northern Wisconsin woods, Alec and Rachel discussed the Bible and homosexuality. But I can easily see Alec resorting to the same kind of arguments made by gay activists and their supporters in clerical garb.

We never discussed what the Bible said about homosexuality. When I was first getting to know him, I was puzzled by his spiritual beliefs regarding Christianity. In the religious world of my upbringing, people were divided into two camps: those who were genuine Christians and the "lost." We expected to be able to see the fruit of the Spirit evident in Christians, as commanded in the New Testament: "The fruit of the Spirit is love, joy, peace, patience, kindness, generosity, faithfulness, gentleness and self-control. There is no law against such things" (Gal. 5:22–23 NRSV).

Alec certainly appeared to exhibit the fruit of the Spirit in his life. He was kind and loving and seemed to be at peace with himself and the world. But he also didn't use the evangelical code words that would clearly identify him as "one of us." When I attempted to pin him down regarding spiritual matters, his answers were more confusing than reassuring although he claimed he believed the same theological doctrines I did.

However, even as he affirmed his Christian beliefs, Alec hastened to add that he considered himself an "idealist." He described his philosophy in rather arcane terms that I, in my fledgling theological and philosophical understanding, had difficulty grasping. I recall little of his lofty discourse about striving for the human potential that existed in each of us. I wondered if he fully understood it all himself. It seemed that his philosophical talk was his way of affirming that his religious beliefs transcended "mere" Christianity. A little warning bell went off in my head: why was Alec careful to distinguish himself from historic, orthodox Christianity? In time I realized that his secret homosexual lifestyle prevented Alec from unambiguously identifying himself as a Christian.

I also realized, by his arguments the evening he shared his true intentions toward me, that Alec accepted the "weighing in the balance" view of salvation—that God will judge our good deeds on one side of a scale and our bad deeds on the other. If our good deeds outweigh our bad deeds, we go to heaven.

No biblical justification exists for this view. While the Bible says that every person will be judged "according to the deeds done in the flesh," it doesn't say people's good deeds will be weighed against their bad deeds. Instead, there is only one criterion for entering heaven: being "washed in the blood" of Jesus Christ the Redeemer. It is Jesus' sacrificial death on the cross that pays the penalty for our sins, and only those who confess Jesus Christ as Lord and Savior will enter heaven.

My church background and theological training emphasized personal salvation through faith alone in Jesus Christ as Savior. The corollary doctrine was that of eternal security, which means that true believers can never "lose" their salvation. My background also supplied an aversion to the unbiblical teaching of "salvation by works," which was good for perspective but sometimes had the unintended effect of downplaying the importance of a believer exhibiting "good works" in life. Properly understood, exhibiting good works is not a means to salvation, but an obedient response to Jesus as Lord and to the commands of the gospel.

Years later I came to appreciate the importance of not only professing Christianity but also living the Christian faith. The importance of both belief and obedient activity has come to the fore in recent years as homosexual supporters assert that one can be a Christian while engaging in homosexual behavior. Alec doubtlessly would have agreed with such a view. Let's consider this radical misinterpretation of sexual morals taught to Christians since the first century.

The Gay Agenda to Change Christian Teaching

Gay activists and their supporters have increased the acceptance of the homosexual lifestyle on a number of fronts: in the courts, the classroom, and the entertainment industry. Yet all this is not enough. Those advocating the full acceptance of homosexuality realize that despite their success in the public arena, one bulwark against their agenda remains: the considerable moral influence of Christian denominations and churches across the land.

To overcome this opposition, concerted efforts are being made to show that homosexuality is fully compatible with Christian beliefs and practices. *Such activists are called "revisionists" because their goal is to revise—or redefine—the historic teaching of the Christian church regarding sexual behavior.* These activists are well aware that if they win the battle against the churches, they will achieve a cultural triumph more strategic than any political or legal battle thus far.

The homosexual activist organization Human Rights Campaign (HRC) issued a report titled "Mixed Blessings," which claims there is no "clear answer" to the issue of homosexuality in the church, only "growing questions, controversies, and uncertainties." According to the report, "There is no single religious view about gay and lesbian people. Nor is there one set of answers to the questions, Is gay and lesbian sex a sin? Should ministers and rabbis bless gay and lesbian unions?"[1]

Homosexual apologists falsely assume that because some churches and theologians accept homosexual behavior, this "proves" that historic Christian teaching is somehow in question. *On the contrary, the moral status of homosexual behavior is not determined by current notions about sexuality but by the revealed truths of Scripture buttressed by nearly two thousand years of Christian tradition.*

True to its name, the HRC report "Mixed Blessings" was far from unmitigated good news for the homosexual agenda. The report could not conceal the fact that despite efforts to promote the acceptance of homosexuality within the church, the major denominations remain surprisingly resilient. With the exception of a few smaller religious bodies such as the Unitarian Universalist Association and Reform Judaism, to date the major denominations have continued to affirm that homosexual behavior is outside the realm of appropriate Christian conduct (see appendix).

Only the United Church of Christ, which defers the issue to regional associations and local congregations, and the Episcopal Church, whose position is ambiguous, appear to be faltering. Nevertheless, the battles continue, as those who favor homosexuality continue to challenge the biblical, theological, and constitutional standards of their respective denominations.

How Revisionists Attempt to Prove Their Case

For revisionists to argue that homosexuality is a "gift" from God they must first show that the Bible does not condemn such behavior. Thus, a three-tiered strategy is employed to explain the biblical passages that condemn homosexual behavior:

1. Exegetical: (For our purposes, "exegesis" refers to determining the literal meaning of the Hebrew and Greek biblical texts.) Revisionists attempt to show that such biblical texts do not actually refer to homosexuality or at best are intended to condemn only an "abusive" form of homosexuality.

2. Historical: Once it becomes clear, as it inevitably does, that Scripture does condemn homosexual behavior, attention then shifts to the second or "historical" line of attack. On this level revisionists concede that the biblical passages indeed condemn homosexuality. However, they then argue that the biblical writers are only reflecting "culturally conditioned" moral beliefs of a pre-scientific age that are no longer relevant.

3. Theological: When it becomes clear that the biblical teaching regarding human sexuality cannot simply be dismissed as culturally irrelevant, there remains one final line of argumentation: an appeal is made to an overarching theological ethic—such as the presence of "love," "commitment," or "mutuality"—that allegedly trumps explicit moral imperatives and justifies homosexual relationships.

Since what the Bible has to say about homosexuality is—or should be—of great significance to Christians, we will look at passages in the Old and New Testaments that address this moral issue. We will then look at some of the "historical" arguments that claim these texts are no longer relevant. Finally, we will evaluate the claim that certain "theological" motifs take precedence over specific moral prohibitions in the biblical text.

We will attempt to answer the question, Is homosexuality a divine "gift" to be "celebrated" or immoral behavior that is rejected by Scripture and tradition?

Let's begin our examination of the three levels of argumentation used by revisionists as "proof" that the Bible does not condemn homosexuality. We will first present the revisionist argument and then follow with a refutation of that argument.

Exegetical Arguments

Genesis 19—The Sodom Story

Before they had gone to bed, all the men from every part of the city of Sodom—both young and old—surrounded the house. They called to Lot, "Where are the men who came to you tonight? Bring them out to us so that we can have sex with [*yada'*] them."

Lot went outside to meet them and shut the door behind him and said, "No, my friends. Don't do this wicked thing. Look, I have two daughters who have never slept [*yada'*] with a man. Let me bring them out to you, and you can do what you like with them. But don't do anything to these men, for they have come under the protection of my roof."

"Get out of our way," they replied. And they said, "This fellow came here as an alien, and now he wants to play the judge! We'll treat you worse than them." They kept bringing pressure on Lot and moved forward to break down the door. (Gen. 19:4–9 NIV)

REVISIONIST ARGUMENT

In 1955 Anglican priest Derrick Sherwin Bailey advanced a novel interpretation of Genesis 19 that has been used by homosexual activists to deny that the sin of Sodom was homosexuality. Bailey's argument was based on the King James Version, which states in verse 5 that the men of Sodom demanded that Lot bring out his visitors "that we may know them." Bailey suggested that the opposition to homosexuality in Christian tradition was based upon a mistranslation of the Hebrew word translated "to know" (*yada'*).[2]

According to Bailey's theory, *yada'* does not refer to the desire of the Sodomites to have sexual relations with Lot's angelic visitors, who the inhabitants of the city apparently mistook for men. Rather, Bailey claims that the Sodomites merely intended to "get acquainted with" and to "examine the credentials" of Lot's visitors. To support this interpretation, Bailey points out that in only 10 (there are actually at least 15) of 943 occurrences of *yada'* in the Old Testament is the word used to refer to sexual intercourse. Sodom's sin, according to Bailey, was that the men of the city reacted with violence, thus causing a "breach [of] the rules of hospitality."[3]

As we shall see, revisionists often disagree about how they interpret the various biblical texts dealing with homosexuality. In this passage, other revisionists argue that the offense committed by the men of Sodom was their intention to commit homosexual rape. Peter J. Gomes of Harvard Divinity School states the implications of this interpretation: "The attempted homosexual rape of the angels at Lot's door, while vivid and distasteful, is hardly the subject of the story or the cause of the punishment. . . . Homosexual rape is never to be condoned; it is indeed, like heterosexual rape, an abomination before God. This instance of attempted homosexual rape, however, does not invalidate all homosexuals or all homosexual activity."[4]

RESPONSE

The context determines meaning. Bailey's argument sounds impressive, but statistics are of little use in translating words in a particular context. The meaning of a word is determined by the immediate passage, and the Sodom story leaves little doubt that the Sodomites were intent upon having sexual relations with Lot's visitors. This interpretation is so compelling that even revisionist scholar Robin Scroggs is forced to conclude that "it seems to me difficult to deny the sexual intent of the Sodomites. I still believe the traditional interpretation to be correct."[5]

Bailey contradicts his own theory, by admitting yada' *refers to sexual relations in the passage.* The word *yada'* is used twice in the passage, and in the second occurrence—where Lot offers his two daughters who have "never slept with (*yada'*) a man"—the word has an unambiguous sexual meaning. Ironically, even Bailey admits this although it contradicts his own "statistical" theory. This constitutes strong contextual evidence that the first occurrence, where the men of Sodom seek to "know" the angels, also has a sexual meaning.

The "inhospitality" argument defies logic. If the men of Sodom were only interested in "examining the credentials" of Lot's visitors, why would Lot defensively shut the door behind him as he confronted the Sodomites, appealing to them to not do "this wicked thing"? That their demands were sexual is clear by Lot's offering his two virgin daughters to the men, adding resignedly, "and you can do what you like with them."

Other passages confirm the sexual depravity of Sodom. Ezekiel 16:49–50 condemns the men of Sodom, stating that they "committed abomination before Me; therefore I took them away as I saw fit" (NKJV). The word *abomination* is *to'ebah,* which signifies the gravest moral censure possible in ancient Hebrew. Nowhere in the Old Testament is inhospitality listed as an abomination, unlike homosexual behavior (see Lev. 18:22). In addition, the New Testament Book of Jude states that Sodom and Gomorrah had "given themselves over to sexual immorality and gone after strange flesh . . . suffering the vengeance of eternal fire" (v. 7 NKJV).

The initial intent of the Sodomites was not to rape but to have sexual relations with Lot's visitors. In what may have been the debauched ancient equivalent of "Let's party!" the men of the city called out to Lot: "Where are the men who came to you tonight? Bring them out to us so that we can have sex with (*yada'*) them." It was only after the Sodomites were rebuffed that they became violent. The rampant homosexuality of the men of Sodom constituted a primary reason for the city's judgment, as indicated by the Lord to Abraham: "How great is the outcry against Sodom and Gomorrah and how very grave their sin!"

(Gen. 18:20 NRSV). The fact that the men of Sodom were intent upon having homosexual relations with Lot's visitors, even to the point of force, does not reduce their crime to merely the use of force.

Judges 19–21—The Outrage at Gibeah

While they were enjoying themselves, some of the wicked men of the city surrounded the house. Pounding on the door, they shouted to the old man who owned the house, "Bring out the man who came to your house so we can have sex with him."

The owner of the house went outside and said to them, "No, my friends, don't be so vile. Since this man is my guest don't do this disgraceful thing. Look, here is my virgin daughter and his concubine. I will bring them out to you now, and you can use them and do to them whatever you wish. But to this man, don't do such a disgraceful thing."

But the men would not listen to him. So the man took his concubine and sent her outside to them, and they raped her and abused her throughout the night, and at dawn they let her go. At daybreak the woman went back to the house where her master was staying, fell down at the door and lay there until daylight. (Judg. 19:22–26 NIV)

REVISIONIST ARGUMENT

As with the Sodom story, revisionist scholars typically deny any sexual intent on the part of the men of Gibeah. Bailey questions the sexual interpretation of the Hebrew word *nebalah* in the passage, claiming that the reference to "folly" (in our translation, "disgraceful thing") "need be nothing more than a rhetorical addition designed to emphasize the deplorable lack of courtesy shown by the Gibeathites toward the visitor."[6]

RESPONSE

The sexual meaning of yada'. Here, as at Sodom, the men of the city demand that the visitor be brought out so that they might "have sex with" (*yada'*) him. The word *yada'* ("have sex with") in the above translation removes any ambiguity caused by the circumlocution "to know them." As in the Sodom story, at Gibeah we see the unchivalrous offering of women to the townsmen in a desperate attempt to prevent the outrage of homosexual relations compounded by violence.

Nebalah *refers to sexual offenses.* Bailey ignores his own "statistical argument," as the majority of occurrences of *nebalah* in the Hebrew Bible refer to sexual offenses, a fact that Bailey himself admits.[7] The use of this term confirms that the issue is not one of hospitality but rather the desire of the men to have homosexual relations with the Levite.

An inescapable conclusion. Revisionist scholars themselves admit that the outrage at Gibeah involved homosexuality. Harold I. Haas notes, "No one seems to make much of this event for understanding the Sodom story, but it surely suggests a sexual rather than a social customs interpretation of so close a parallel as the Sodom story."[8] Similarly, David L. Bartlett, writing in *Homosexuality and the Christian Faith,* concludes that "it takes special imaginative power to believe, as Bailey does, that what the men of Gibeah were after was the acquaintance of the visiting men, or that the old man offered his virgin daughter and the other's concubine only to protect his rights of hospitality."[9]

The Gibeah passage confirms the sexual interpretation of the Sodom story in several key aspects. The textual evidence from the two stories indicates that those cities were inhabited by men so sexually depraved that they were prepared to sexually violate not only males (which they evidently preferred) but whoever was made available to them.

Leviticus 18:22; 20:13—The Mosaic Law

You shall not lie with a male as with a woman. It is an abomination. (Lev. 18:22 NKJV)

If a man lies with a male as he lies with a woman, both of them have committed an abomination. They shall surely be put to death. Their blood shall be upon them. (Lev. 20:13 NKJV)

REVISIONIST ARGUMENT

Since it is generally conceded that on the exegetical level the above passages in Leviticus do condemn homosexuality, these passages will be discussed more fully in the section dealing with historical arguments. However, there is one argument put forth by revisionists: "In these passages acts are condemned not because of some intrinsic aberration but because of their association with idolatry (particularly, in the sexual references, to Canaanite idolatry)."[10] This argument contends that Leviticus condemns only that homosexual behavior that is associated with idolatry.

RESPONSE

Leviticus addresses homosexual acts in general. A comparison of the two texts indicates that Deuteronomy is concerned with *sacred* sodomy, while Leviticus is concerned with *secular* sodomy. The technical terms for female (*qedeshah*) and male (*qadesh*) cultic prostitution are absent in the Leviticus condemnation. Instead, we find an unambiguous and generic description of the homosexual act: "You shall not lie with a male as with a woman." No evidence shows that Leviticus intends to limit the condemnation of homosexuality to that of an idolatrous context.

Other passages specifically address ritual homosexuality. Passages such as Deuteronomy 23:17 (see discussion below) address the ritual homosexual prostitution that was common to Canaanite religion: "There shall be no ritual harlot [*qedeshah*] of the daughters of Israel, or a perverted one [*qadesh*] of the sons of Israel"(NKJV).[11] By contrast, Leviticus does not limit its condemnation of homosexuality in only a ritual context.

Leviticus permits no exceptions. Leviticus makes no mention of any mitigating circumstances that would permit homosexual behavior, such as within the context of a "loving, committed relationship." Bailey himself is forced to conclude: "It is hardly open to doubt that both the laws in Leviticus relate to ordinary homosexual acts between men, and not to ritual or other acts performed in the name of religion."[12]

The revisionary argument is logically inconsistent. Finally, the revisionist argument leads to a logical impasse: if homosexuality is to be condemned *only* when practiced in an idolatrous context, then the same is true for the other prohibited behaviors listed in the immediate passage. As P. Michael Ukleja writes, "To hold to such a distinction, one would have to conclude that adultery was not morally wrong (18:20), child sacrifice had no moral implications (18:21), and that nothing is inherently evil with bestiality (18:23)."[13]

Deuteronomy 23:17–18—Cultic Prostitution in Ancient Israel

> None of the daughters of Israel shall be a temple prostitute [*qedeshah*]; none of the sons of Israel shall be a temple prostitute [*qadesh*]. You shall not bring the fee of a prostitute or the wages of a male prostitute into the house of the LORD your God in payment for any vow, for both of these are abhorrent to the LORD your God. (Deut. 23:17–18 NRSV)

REVISIONIST ARGUMENT

Despite the rendering of *qadesh* as "Sodomite" in some translations, revisionists deny that the term refers to a male homosexual. They view the *qadesh* as the male counterpart of the female *qedeshah:* as the *qedeshah* solicits intercourse with males, the *qadesh* engages in ritual intercourse with the female devotees of the temple. Thus if *qadesh* does not refer to homosexual practices, it is irrelevant to the discussion.

RESPONSE

Evidence from the Greek Septuagint. The ancient Greek translation of the Hebrew Bible, known as the Septuagint, indicates that *qadesh* engaged in homosexual conduct. The Septuagint uses several words to translate *qadesh,* but of special interest is *endiellagmenos,* "one who has changed his nature," used in 1 Kings 22:46. In this passage the Hebrew *qadesh* is translated *endiellagmenos.*

Connection with transsexuality. In addition, the eminent biblical scholar of the last century, S. R. Driver, while commenting on cultic prostitution in Deuteronomy 23:17–18, relates *endiellagmenos* to Deuteronomy 22:5, which states, "A woman shall not wear man's clothing, nor shall a man put on a woman's clothing; for whoever does these things is an abomination [*to'ebah*] to the LORD your God" (NASB).[14] Here the transsexual implications of the verse are evident. In addition, the use of *to'ebah* indicates the passage is concerned with grave moral transgressions.

It is likely that Deuteronomy 22:5 is referring to a particular variant of homosexual practice, that of transvestism—the adoption of the dress and behavior of the opposite sex. Thus Driver connects the homosexual practice of transvestism with the practice of male cultic prostitution—considered an "abomination" by the Hebrew text. Accordingly, the *qadesh* were likely male prostitutes who engaged in homosexual acts with the male devotees of the temple and may also have been transvestites.

1 Samuel 18–20 and 2 Samuel 1:26— David and Jonathan

After David had finished talking with Saul, Jonathan became one in spirit with David, and he loved him as himself. (1 Sam. 18:1 NIV)

But Jonathan was very fond of David. (1 Sam. 19:1 NIV)

But David took an oath and said, "Your father knows very well that I have found favor in your eyes." . . . Then they kissed each other and wept together—but David wept the most. (1 Sam. 20:3 and 41 NIV)

"I grieve for you, Jonathan my brother; you were very dear to me. Your love was wonderful, more wonderful than that of women." (2 Sam. 1:26 NIV)

REVISIONIST ARGUMENT

Most revisionists, realizing they are pushing the envelope with this one, remain tentative in their suggestions that the future king of Israel was involved in a homosexual relationship with King Saul's son, Jonathan. Others seriously postulate that David and Jonathan can serve as a prototype for modern homosexual unions.[15]

RESPONSE

"Love" is not to be equated with "sex." The revisionist argument regarding David and Jonathan highlights the chronic and mistaken tendency among homosexual apologists to assume that all loving human relationships should be open to sexual expression. This constitutes a perversion of the noble ideal of true friendship, twisting it into base lust. As Anton N. Marco writes, such activists "virtually deny the possibility that true nonsexual intimacy can exist between persons of the same gender, which would almost deny the possibility of the existence of true friend-

ship."[16] To inject a sexual component into any loving human relationships outside of marriage—including those between parents and children, siblings, as well as friendships—would be both morally wrong and destructive.

There is no sexual connotation in the Hebrew texts. First Samuel 19:1 says that Jonathan "was very fond of" David. The Hebrew word used here (*chaphets*) means "joy of the heart" and is never used in the Hebrew Bible to denote sexuality. Similarly, the phrase "became one in spirit" (1 Sam. 18:1) signified the depth of sincere friendship between David and Jonathan. The same is commanded of believers in the church (Phil. 1:27). Note that 1 Samuel 18:1 does *not* say David and Jonathan became "one flesh," which signifies the unity reserved for a man and a woman within marriage (Gen. 2:24 and Eph. 5:31).

The revisionist argument shows an ignorance of Middle Eastern culture. The references that David and Jonathan "kissed each other" during their tearful parting do not signify romantic or erotic kissing. In the ancient Middle East, as well as today, family members and friends greet each other with a kiss on each cheek, a custom that has no sexual connotation. This venerated custom, also common throughout Europe and elsewhere, is reflected in the New Testament command: "Greet all the brothers and sisters with a holy kiss" (1 Thess. 5:26 NRSV).

There is a love that is greater than sexual love. David's description of his love for Jonathan as "more wonderful than that of women" speaks of the wonderful blessing that is deep human friendship. David considered the love shared between friends to be even more meaningful than sexual love. Friendship is an essential form of meaningful human affection blessed by God, which does not in any way denigrate the love between husband and wife. Tragically, those who equate "love" and "sex" by sexualizing their relationships destroy the possibility of genuine friendship, crossing boundaries never meant to be crossed except in marriage.

Romans 1:24–32—Unnatural Sexual Relations

Therefore God gave them over in the sinful desires of their hearts to sexual impurity for the degrading of their bodies with one another. They exchanged the truth of God for a lie, and worshiped and served created things rather than the Creator—who is forever praised. Amen.

Because of this, God gave them over to shameful lusts. Even their women exchanged natural relations for unnatural ones. In the same way the men also abandoned natural relations with women and were inflamed with lust for one another. Men committed indecent acts with other men, and received in themselves the due penalty for their perversion.

Furthermore, since they did not think it worthwhile to retain the knowledge of God, he gave them over to a depraved mind, to do what ought not to be done. They have become filled with every kind of wickedness, evil, greed and depravity. They are full of envy, murder, strife, deceit and malice. They are gossips, slanderers, God-haters, insolent, arrogant and boastful; they invent ways of doing evil; they disobey their parents; they are senseless, faithless, heartless, ruthless. Although they know God's righteous decree that those who do such things deserve death, they not only continue to do these very things but also approve of those who practice them." (Rom. 1:24–32 NIV)

Revisionist Argument

While admitting that this passage contains an explicit description of homosexual acts, revisionists nonetheless argue that Paul did not intend to condemn homosexuality *per se.* Revisionist New Testament scholar Robin Scroggs holds that for the writers of the New Testament there was only one model of homosexuality—that of pederasty (sexual relations between an adult and a child): "Thus what the New Testament was against was the image of homosexuality as pederasty and primarily here in its more sordid and dehumanizing dimensions."[17]

This argument resembles the "homosexual rape" argument used by revisionists in the Sodom story, in that it limits the prohibition of an immoral behavior to the "abusive excesses" of that behavior. According to this argument, the biblical writer intends to oppose both homosexual and heterosexual abuses (pederasty)—without condemning the "legitimate" forms of either (sexual relations between consenting adults). As Scroggs puts it, "If he [Paul] opposed something specific, then his statements cannot be generalized beyond the limitations of his intentionality without violating the integrity of the Scripture."[18]

In a variation of the "abusive excesses" argument, author Tony Campolo attempts to limit Paul's condemnation to "abusive" homosexual behavior: "Paul, in Romans 1, condemned one kind of homosexual behavior which is a perversion resulting from an insatiable sexual appetite yielded to the demonic."[19] Campolo goes on to claim, "But there are other causes for homosexual behavior . . . I do not believe that Paul was dealing with them, and thus his condemnations do not apply to them."[20]

RESPONSE

Paul allows no mitigating circumstances. As with the "homosexual rape" argument discussed earlier, Scroggs and Campolo fail to adequately account for the biblical text. Romans 1 gives no indication that Paul is referring solely to pederasty. To the contrary, he condemns homosexual behavior with no qualifications and exceptions whatsoever.

The condemnation is not limited to pederasty. Contrary to Scroggs, Paul is not addressing homosexual acts between men and boys: the text specifically condemns homosexual acts between *adults.* To support his thesis, Scroggs cites a reference in the writings of first-century Jewish philosopher Philo, where Philo uses "the 'male and male' terminology when he is explicitly referring to pederasty."[21] However, the passage in Philo's *The Contemplative Life* that Scroggs refers to continues with the phrase "differing only in age."[22] Thus, Philo explicitly qualifies his use of "males having sexual relations with males" terminology to clarify that he is referring to pederasty. Paul makes no such clarification to indicate that he is condemning only pederasty.

Paul does not allow for "loving" homosexual acts. Campolo suggests that there may be forms of homosexual expression that do not fall under Paul's condemnation, despite the complete absence of scriptural evidence. But as Bishop Bennett J. Sims notes, "The logical effect of the exemption argument is to suggest that, given the proper motivation, there are loving ways to be 'full of envy, murder, strife, deceit, malignity . . .' (Rom. 1:29). This is moral absurdity."[23]

Paul does not intend to distinguish between "moral" and immoral homosexual acts. If indeed there were a commendable expression of homosexuality, we would expect Paul to distinguish between such an expression and the immoral expressions of homosexuality, as he did with other ethical issues. Regarding the eating of food offered to idols, Paul carefully explains the circumstances under which it is proper to partake of such food and when it is not (1 Cor. 8:7–13; 10:19–31). Paul makes similar distinctions when he grants the "Pauline privilege" regarding the dissolution of marriage between a Christian and an unbeliever (1 Cor. 7:10–17).

1 Corinthians 6:9–11—Male Prostitutes and Homosexual Offenders

> Do you not know that the wicked will not inherit
> the kingdom of God? Do not be deceived: Neither the

sexually immoral nor idolaters nor adulterers nor male prostitutes nor homosexual offenders nor thieves nor the greedy nor drunkards nor slanderers will inherit the kingdom of God. And that is what some of you were. But you were washed, you were sanctified, you were justified in the name of the Lord Jesus Christ and by the Spirit of our God. (1 Cor. 6:9–10 NIV)

REVISIONIST ARGUMENT

The vice list of 1 Corinthians 6:9–10 contains two Greek terms relevant to the discussion about the Bible and homosexuality: *malakos,* translated "male prostitutes," and *arsenokoitai,* translated "homosexual offenders." Revisionists claim that neither of these terms refers to homosexuality. John Boswell argues that *arsenokoitai* means "male sexual agents, i.e., active male prostitutes, who were common throughout the Hellenistic world in the time of Paul."[24] Robin Scroggs, on the other hand, argues that the term refers to the active partner in a pederastic relationship.[25] Both agree that the term cannot be used to justify a general condemnation of homosexuality.

With regard to *malakos,* Boswell argues that the term "refers to general moral weakness, with no specific connection to homosexuality."[26] Scroggs, in keeping with his insistence that *arsenokoitai* refers to pederasty, also argues for a narrow interpretation of the term: "Thus the use of *malakos* would almost certainly conjure up images of the effeminate call boy *if* the context otherwise suggested some form of pederasty."[27]

RESPONSE

Arsenokoitai *refers to all manner of homosexual acts.* The etymology of *arsenokoitai* does not indicate that only one kind of homosexuality is in view. The Arndt-Gingrich Greek lexicon translates the term as "a male who practices homosexuality, pederast, sodomite," and refers the reader to Romans 1:27, which as

we have seen is a generic description of homosexual acts.[28] Several
Greek lexicons follow Arndt-Gingrich in defining *arsenokoitai* as
referring generally to homosexuality, ignoring the fine distinctions that are pivotal to the revisionist arguments.[29]

Arsenokoitai *is the Greek equivalent to the Hebrew* mishkab
zakur. Scroggs correctly identifies *arsenokoitai* with the Hebrew
mishkab zakur ("males lying with males"), the term used in
Leviticus to describe homosexual acts. As in Romans 1, here
Scroggs incorrectly limits the biblical prohibition to pederasty.
However, that Paul would interpret *arsenokoitai* with the Hebrew
mishkab zakur is entirely in keeping with his rabbinic background, especially given that both terms have the same literal
meaning: "males lying with males."

Evidence from the Septuagint that arsenokoitai *refers to homosexual acts.* The Septuagint, dating from around 250 B.C., uses the
two words that compose *arsenokoitai* in its translation of both
Leviticus 18:22 and 20:13. The latter passage, for example, contains the phrase *"meta arsenos koiten gunaikos"* ("to lie with a man
as with a woman"). This constitutes important evidence because
the Septuagint was widely used by Jews in lands where Greek was
spoken. The apostle Paul, born and educated in Greek Antioch,
was referring to the unqualified prohibition of homosexual acts in
Leviticus when he used *arsenokoitai* in 1 Corinthians 6:9.

Malakos *is also used in reference to homosexuality.* Contrary to
Boswell, in the ancient literature *malakos* appears in the context of
homosexuality. Boswell himself admits that the term "is sometimes
applied to obviously gay persons."[30] Scroggs also sees that the term
refers to homosexual practice, although once again he attempts to
limit the meaning to "the general practice of pederasty."[31]

Greek philosophers used malakos *to refer specifically to the
passive homosexual partner.* In his *Problems,* Aristotle uses *malakos*
to describe passive homosexual behavior.[32] Dionysius of
Halicarnassus also connects the term with passive male homo-

sexuality in his *Roman Antiquities,* where he gives as one definition of *malakos* someone who "had been 'effeminate' as a child and had undergone the things associated with women."[33]

Similarly, the first-century Jewish philosopher Philo uses malakia *to refer to passive homosexual behavior.* Robert A. J. Gagnon, in *The Bible and Homosexual Practice,* notes that Philo uses *malakia* (a cognate of *malakos*) "to refer to the passive homosexual partners (*hoi paschontes*) who cultivate feminine features." Gagnon further notes that "Philo uses the word *malakotes* ('softness, luxury, decadence') to denote the whole feminizing process of receptive male partners in homosexual intercourse."[34]

Distinction between arsenokoitai *and* malakos. Although the two terms both refer generally to male homosexuality, their appearance together in 1 Corinthians 6:9 indicates a difference in emphasis. Bartlett suggests that *arsenokoitai* signifies "men who have intercourse with males, specifically 'sodomites' in the narrower sense of one who takes the active role in male homosexual intercourse."[35] With regard to *malakos,* Arndt-Gingrich concludes that the term refers to "men and boys who allow themselves to be misused homosexually."[36] As Hans Lietzmann summarizes, "Ein *malakos* ist das Passivim zum *arsenokoitas* (a *malakos* is the passive sexual partner of an *arsenokoitas*)."[37]

Conclusion: Exegetical Arguments

It is ironic that, after the revisionist arguments are played out, it is the revisionists themselves who often freely admit the failure of such efforts. John von Rohr, while attempting a "theology of homosexuality," admits that "the fact still remains that where the Bible does explicitly refer to this matter it is condemnatory in its judgment."[38]

Others, such as Thomas Maurer, oppose efforts to reinterpret the biblical texts relating to homosexuality: "Even more annoying to me is Rohr's attempt to rationalize condemnatory statements in the Bible about homosexuality." For Mauer, the question is instead, "Why don't we have the courage and the candor to admit that the attitudes and opinions expressed by these ancient writers are thoroughly reprehensible and repugnant and were so even in their time, not to mention in this supposedly enlightened day?"[39]

Mauer's comments bring us to the second level of our discussion: the attempt to show that the biblical texts condemning homosexuality are no longer valid and binding upon Christians.

CHAPTER 5

Historical Arguments

WHEN IT BECOMES clear that the biblical texts indeed do condemn homosexuality, revisionists have a second line of attack: to argue that the biblical teaching regarding homosexuality is the product of a pre-scientific age—culturally and historically limited to that earlier time—and is therefore not binding upon those living in the modern world.

This approach is typified by the study *Human Sexuality: New Directions in American Catholic Thought,* commissioned by the Catholic Theological Society of America (CTSA).[1] The study was censured by the Vatican and eventually by the CTSA itself for its rejection of the traditional understanding regarding sexual ethics. I refer to it here only as an illustration of revisionist thinking on the "historical" level—certainly not as representative of authentic Catholic teaching.

In discussing the issue of homosexuality, the study concedes that, on the exegetical level, "there is no doubt but that the Old Testament condemns homosexual practice with the utmost severity." However, the report then asserts that "simply citing verses from the Bible outside of their historical context and then blithely applying them to homosexuals today does grave injustice both to Scripture and to people who have already suffered a great deal from the travesty of biblical interpretation."[2]

This inconsistent claim denies the contemporary relevance of biblical texts that discuss homosexuality. Let's look at the revisionist "historical" claims regarding the biblical texts that refer to homosexuality.

Rejecting the Authority of the Levitical Law

Revisionist Historical Argument

One writer expresses the "consistency" argument by stating that "a highly selective kind of biblical interpretation would be required to hold that these two verses in the Holiness Code are absolutely binding on Christians. Much of the Holiness Code, including the rules for sacrifice and the dietary regulations, is ignored by almost all Christians in their ethical reflection."[3]

Thus, in the revisionist argument, we are faced with the choice of either consistently holding to *all* of the Levitical prohibitions—including the civil or ceremonial laws—or admitting that the Old Testament law in its entirety is no longer binding upon Christians.

Another revisionist argument is to claim that the Levitical law has been superseded by grace, as Mark Olson writes, "But for followers of Jesus, the Levitical code is no longer applicable in any literal sense. Paul reminds us that we live not under law but grace."[4]

Response

Revisionists ignore distinctions in the Levitical law. The revisionist argument fails to account for the various kinds of laws, including the difference between the moral and the civil or ceremonial laws. That such distinctions exist is clear from the severity of the punishment for violations of the moral law, contrasted with the comparatively lenient punishment for infractions of the civil or ceremonial law.

Jesus confirms distinctions in the Old Testament Law. Jesus castigated the scribes and Pharisees for strictly adhering to the ceremonial law, while neglecting "the weightier provisions of the law" (Matt. 23:23 NASB). Walter Kaiser observes that these words of Jesus "should be an eternal answer to all who find it difficult to distinguish between the moral, civil, and ceremonial elements of the law."[5] In addition, the Levitical texts that discuss sexual transgressions are an extension of the Seventh Commandment, the prohibition of adultery, as Anthony Phillips states, "Leviticus 20:11 can be isolated as the first stage of the reinterpretation of the crime of adultery to include all unnatural sexual unions."[6]

Homosexuality is classed with the most severe offences. Grave moral transgressions are considered capital offences and incur the death penalty. These include murder (Exod. 21:12); violent kidnapping (Deut. 24:7); idolatry (Exod. 22:20); adultery (Lev. 20:10); incest (Lev. 20:11–12, 14); rape (Deut. 22:25); bestiality (Lev. 20:15); and homosexuality (Lev. 20:13).

The moral law is binding for Christians. In contrast to the civil or ceremonial laws, the Ten Commandments have enduring relevancy for Christians. Jesus declared, "Do not think that I have come to abolish the law or the prophets; I have come not to abolish but to fulfill" (Matt. 5:17 NRSV). The ceremonial law, including animal sacrifice for the atonement of sins, was fulfilled in the sacrificial death of Jesus Christ and has been done away with. However, in the New Testament there is no corresponding "fulfillment" (and thus abrogation) of the moral law.

The apostle Paul affirms the continued authority of the moral law. In Romans 3:31, Paul concludes a discourse about the relationship between law and grace by asking, "Do we then nullify the Law through faith? May it never be! On the contrary, we establish the Law" (NASB). In a subsequent discussion about the usefulness of the law, he states, "So then, the Law is holy, and the commandment is holy and righteous and good" (Rom. 7:12 NASB).

Salvation is from the transgression of the law, not from the moral authority of the law itself.

By contrast, the civil or ceremonial laws have been done away with. The New Testament explicitly rejects the continued obedience to ceremonial laws. Jesus set aside the dietary laws, declaring that "whatever goes into the man from outside cannot defile him; because it does not go into his heart, but into his stomach, and is eliminated." Mark then adds, "Thus He declared all foods clean" (7:18–19 NASB). In 1 Corinthians 6:12–20, the continued validity of the moral law is affirmed while the dietary laws are discarded: "Food is for the stomach, and the stomach is for food; but God will do away with both of them. Yet the body is not for immorality, but for the Lord" (v. 13 NASB).

Denying the continued authority of the law is "lawlessness." The revisionist effort to deny any relevance to the law manifests an antinomianism that is contrary to the gospel. Paul addressed this attitude when he discussed the meaning of the grace of God: "What shall we say then? Are we to continue in sin that grace might increase? May it never be! How shall we who died to sin still live in it?" (Rom. 6:1–2 NASB). J. Murray rightly summarizes: "The conclusion is inescapable that the precepts of the Decalogue have relevance to the believer as the criteria of that manner of life which love to God and to our neighbor dictates."[7]

Denying the Authority of the New Testament

The revisionist arguments on the historical level acknowledge that the New Testament texts condemn homosexual behavior. However, they contend that while those biblical passages may have been valid for an earlier time, they are no longer authoritative for Christians today. The CTSA study states, "St. Paul's moral judgments or statements on sexuality cannot simply be taken out of context and applied to the situations of the present time. They represent the applications of the gospel to the circumstances of the first-century Christian community within the necessarily limited vision of that time."[8]

Revisionist Historical Argument
Regarding "Sexual Orientation"

James Nelson states that "in all probability the biblical writers in each instance were speaking of homosexual acts undertaken by those persons whom the author presumed to be heterosexually constituted."[9] Even the ethicist Helmut Thielicke—a man widely admired by evangelical Protestants—on this point asserts that the possibility of inherent homosexual sexual orientation "must for purely historical reasons be alien to the New Testament."[10] Thus, for Thielicke, the apostle Paul did not intend to make moral judgments regarding such individuals.

Response

Ancient Greek mythology explained "sexual orientation." Historian K. J. Dover, in his *Greek Homosexuality,* mentions evidence indicating that the ancient biblical world was not unaware of the modern concept of "sexual orientation."[11] In the myth of Aristophanes in Plato's *Symposium,* the original sexes are described as created in pairs consisting of a man and a woman, a man and a man, or a woman and a woman.[12] The gods removed one half of the pairs, thus causing the age-old desire to reunite with one's "lost" counterpart. Male homosexual attraction was thought to be caused by a man seeking his lost male counterpart, and lesbianism was caused by a woman seeking her lost feminine half.

Greek philosophy had a concept of "sexual orientation." In discussing Aristotle's *Nicomachean Ethics,* revisionist John Boswell states that Aristotle understood the concept of chronic predisposition toward homosexuality, stating that "Aristotle apparently considered a homosexual disposition perfectly 'natural.'"[13]

Our purpose here is not to validate the beliefs of the ancient Greeks regarding homosexual attraction, but to refute the revisionist argument that the apostle Paul had no understanding of such attraction, and thus did not intend to condemn it. Furthermore, the apostle Paul, who was born and educated in the Greek-speaking world, would have been aware of such beliefs regarding "sexual orientation."

Ancient Jewish and Christian sources also mention same-sex attraction. The first-century Hellenistic-Jewish philosopher Philo describes those who "habituate themselves" to homosexual behavior.[14] The Jewish historian Josephus (A.D. 35–95), in explaining Jewish law regarding marriage, also addresses the phenomenon of those desiring to engage in same-sex behavior: "That law owns no other mixture of sexes but that which nature hath appointed, of a man with his wife, and that this be used only for the procreation of children. But it abhors the mixture of a male with a male; and if any one does that, death is its punishment."[15]

In addition, early church father Clement of Alexandria may also have been referring to same-sex attraction when he spoke of men who "have a natural aversion to a woman; and indeed those who are naturally so constituted do well not to marry."[16]

Revisionists refute their own historical argument. Boswell admits that "the idea that homosexuality represented a congenital physical characteristic was widespread in the Hellenistic world."[17] If this is true, then on what grounds do revisionists assume that Paul was ignorant of the notion of "sexual orientation"? To the contrary, he was well aware of such beliefs, yet made no distinctions in his condemnation of homosexual behavior regardless of one's "sexual orientation."

Revisionist Historical Argument Regarding Modern Science

The findings of modern science must be considered authoritative. Revisionists consider the biblical prohibition of homosexuality to be a relic from a prescientific era, encouraging modern ethicists to take into account the findings of modern science. Walter Wink claims that "the question ceases to be 'what does Scripture command?' and becomes instead 'What is the word that the Spirit speaks to the churches now, in the light of Scripture, tradition, theology, psychology, genetics, anthropology and biology?'"[18]

Response

Seeking scientific "proof" is an inherently impossible endeavor. The difficulties with such an eclectic approach are obvious, and revisionists do not explain how the diverse scientific disciplines are to be correlated into a meaningful guide for ethical decision-making. Revisionists themselves admit that the scientific evidence is in a constant state of flux. In her review of ethical studies, Lisa Cahill comments, "The findings of the human sciences are sometimes circular, sometimes ambiguous, and often in conflict."[19] And as revisionist moral theologian Charles Curran admits, "The ethicist cannot merely follow the majority opinion, for history constantly reminds us that majority opinions are not necessarily true."[20]

There is no scientific consensus regarding the causes of homosexuality. Nowhere is the inability of science to provide answers more evident than in the issue of the cause of homosexuality. As we shall later see, gay activists disagree among themselves about whether homosexuality has a genetic cause. However, all attempts to identify a genetic cause of homosexual behavior have either failed or are inconclusive.[21] In *The Mismeasure of Desire*, homosexual activist Ed Stein makes the case that all attempts to demonstrate a genetic basis for homosexuality have failed.[22]

CHAPTER 6

Theological Arguments

W E HAVE SEEN HOW both the exegetical and the historical arguments of those who would deny the biblical teaching regarding homosexuality are found wanting. But the revisionists are not done yet: they have one last line of argumentation to show that homosexuality is compatible with the Bible. This third and final level shifts the focus away from the traditional biblical passages that discuss homosexuality. Instead, attempts are made to define theological motifs which, when applied to the question of homosexuality, would permit such practices.

Revisionist Theological Argument Regarding the Primacy of Love

The CTSA study states that appropriate sexual behavior must be "self-liberating," "other-enriching," "honest," "faithful," "socially responsible," "life-serving," and "joyous."[1] Homosexual relationships that exhibit these qualities may be judged to be moral. Using another revisionist value, that of "mutuality," Roger Shinn contends, "There have been homosexual relationships with more mutual appreciation than some heterosexual marriages. Any legalistic definition of conditions that make sex 'right' is a trap."[2]

Similarly, the presence of "love" is considered to be the primary criterion for a valid sexual relationship. Homosexual ex-priest John McNeil writes that "a general consideration of human sexuality in the Bible leads to only one certain conclusion: those sexual relations can be justified morally which are a true expression of human love."[3]

Response

The revisionist criterion may be used to justify virtually any sexual relationship. The virtues invoked by revisionists are redefined in a way that alters their original meaning. They are conveniently used to create an illusion of moral substance, when in fact they are quite arbitrary and can be applied to behavior traditionally considered immoral. Thus, for example, W. Dwight Oberholtzer speaks of the "honest one-night stand" and the "faithful (non-marital) lover."[4] In its repudiation of the CTSA report, the Vatican's Sacred Congregation for the Doctrine of the Faith states, "The authors pretend that these are not purely subjective criteria, though in fact they are: the personal judgments about these factors are so different, determined by personal sentiments, feelings, customs, etc., that it would be impossible to single out definite criteria of what exactly integrates a particular person or contributes to his or her creative growth in any specific sexual activity."[5]

True love always acts in accord with objective standards. William Muehl notes, "One of the most popular errors in the realm of Christian ethics has been the effort to make love an omnipotent spiritual quality which has the power to sanctify anything that is done in its name."[6] A subjective definition of "love" leads to moral ambiguity and can never provide a sound basis for ethical evaluation.

As stated by the Sacred Congregation, the goal of true love is properly related to fidelity within marriage: "Such a goal cannot be achieved unless the virtue of conjugal chastity is sincerely practiced."[7] The New Testament specifically rejects subjective ideas of love, calling those who violate the Commandments in the name of "love" liars: "If someone says, 'I love God,' and hates his brother, he is a liar" (v. 20, 1 John 4:7–5:3 NASB).

Revisionists confuse compassion with acceptance of immoral behavior. In an impassioned plea for the acceptance of homosexual practice, Letha Scanzoni declares, "I wish we could say to [homosexuals], 'Yes, I *do* love you—not *in spite of* being a Christian but *because* I am a Christian. The homosexual *is* my neighbor, and I will love my neighbor as myself.'"[8] For Scanzoni, compassion for homosexuals is inseparable from the acceptance of homosexual behavior. But as John Alexander points out, "this same argument could be used to justify racial discrimination. We are to love everyone, including racists. We can't love the sinner without accepting the sin. So (it is permissible) . . . for racists to discriminate in education, housing, and employment."[9] Right? Wrong.

There is an interrelationship between love and law. Revisionists assume a radical separation between the law, which they view as fundamentally repressive, and the "liberating power of love." However, the absolute dichotomy between love and law is not found in the New Testament. Rather they are repeatedly correlated, and revisionists have presented a false distinction between the two.

D. J. Atkinson writes that the real difficulty "is a misconception of the relationship between love and law in the Bible. The biblical understanding of the nature of love is always related to the description or expression of God's character in Himself on the one hand, and the character of life appropriate to the people of God, on the other hand."[10] Jesus affirms this interrelationship between love and law: "If you love me, you will keep my commandments" (John 14:15; also see 15:10 and Matt. 19:17 NRSV).

The Created Order for Human Sexuality

Then God said, "Let us make humankind in our image, according to our likeness"; . . . So God created humankind in his image, in the image of God he created them; male and female he created them. God blessed them, and God said to them, "Be fruitful and multiply, and fill the earth and subdue it" (Gen. 1:26–28 NRSV)

Scripture reveals the divine design for human sexuality. This theme first appears in Genesis 1–3, which describes the creative purposes for male and female. With regard to this passage, Gerhard Von Rad states, "Sexual distinction is also created. The plural in v. 27 ('he created them') is intentionally contrasted with the singular ('him') and prevents one from assuming the creation of an originally androgynous man. By God's will, man was not created alone but designated for the 'thou' of the other sex." Von Rad concludes, "The idea of man . . . finds its full meaning not in the male alone but in man and woman."[11]

This interrelationship is described in Genesis 1:31 as "very good," indicating that the divine intention for human sexuality lies in the mutual interdependence of man and woman. Raymond Collins observes, "Sexual differentiation belongs to the primal plan of the Creator. Human fullness is to be found in the male and female complementarily."[12] While many marriages admittedly fall short of this ideal, homosexual unions are intrinsically flawed and cannot hope to emulate the deep bond that can only occur within a marriage between a man and a woman. "For this reason a man will leave his father and mother and be joined to his wife, and the two will become one flesh (Eph. 5:31 NRSV).

Immediately after the creation of woman we find the establishment of the institution of marriage. The command to "be fruitful and multiply and fill the earth" is given to "male and female," signifying that sexual reproduction and the family properly belong to the heterosexual union. Sexuality finds its rightful place within the bounds of heterosexual marriage. Adultery—which includes all extramarital sexual relations—is a violation of the created order. As Donald J. Keefe writes, "The faith-instinct of the Jewish and the Christian people has found no more profound symbol of the splendor of the good creation than that of feminine beauty, and no more profound symbol of betrayal, the betrayal of the covenant, than marital infidelity."[13] By definition, homosexual acts constitute a "profound symbol of betrayal" of the divine order of creation.

Writing from a Jewish perspective, Hershel J. Matt asks why the Hebrew Scriptures condemned homosexuality and concludes that psychological revulsion or "simply the abhorrence of the unknown" does not sufficiently explain the biblical opposition to homosexuality. According to Matt, "The reasons for the Torah's condemnation must be related rather to the will of the Creator for the human male and female whom He created."[14] The opposition to homosexuality does not arise out of the cultural attitudes of an ancient Near Eastern tribe but originates in the divine will.

Jesus and the Marriage Covenant

It is often claimed by revisionists that Jesus never addressed the issue of homosexuality. Homosexual minister Troy Perry asserts, "As for the question, 'What did Jesus say about homosexuality?' the answer is simple. Jesus said nothing. . . . Jesus was more interested in love."[15] The underlying assumption is that if Jesus did not speak to a certain behavior directly it must not have been important to Him.

The error of such logic can be easily demonstrated. For example, Jesus did not *directly* condemn incest or bestiality either—can we then argue that such practices are therefore acceptable for Christians? The evidence from the Old and New Testaments—as well as from Jewish history and religion—demonstrates that Scripture unambiguously condemns homosexual acts.

This was the cultural and religious heritage of the ancient Jews. Any divergent teaching regarding marriage, family, and human sexuality would have been regarded as scandalous and abhorrent. If Jesus considered homosexuality to be acceptable, one would have expected Him to explicitly state so. That He did not shows that He was fully in agreement with the Hebrew Scriptures and His Jewish heritage. Jesus in fact repeatedly affirmed the continuing relevance and authority of the moral law:

> Do not think that I have come to abolish the law or the prophets; I have come not to abolish but to fulfill. For truly I tell you, until heaven and earth pass away, not one letter, not one stroke of a letter, will pass from the law until all is accomplished. (Matt. 5:17–18 NRSV)

The burden of proof falls on those who desire to show otherwise—and in this regard, arguments based on Jesus' silence are groundless.

Regarding the third and deepest level of theological understanding, Jesus has indeed spoken concerning the nature of human sexuality—and His words directly relate to the issue of homosexuality. When asked about divorce, He quotes from the Book of Genesis, declaring that the marriage covenant is unalterable:

> He answered, "Have you not read that the one who made them at the beginning 'made them male and female,' and said, 'For this reason a man shall leave his father and mother and be joined to his wife, and the two shall become one flesh'? So they are no longer two, but one flesh. Therefore what God has joined together, let no one separate." (Matt. 19:4–6 NRSV)

The "one flesh" teaching of Jesus is reiterated in the apostle Paul's discussion of marriage, where he also quotes Genesis when warning against marital infidelity. Paul states that fleshly immorality violates the spiritual relationship of unity with the Lord:

Do you not know that your bodies are members of Christ? Should I therefore take the members of Christ and make them members of a prostitute? Never!

Do you not know that whoever is united to a prostitute becomes one body with her? For it is said, "The two shall be one flesh." But anyone united to the Lord becomes one spirit with him. Shun fornication! Every sin that a person commits is outside the body; but the fornicator sins against the body itself. (1 Cor. 6:15–18 NRSV)

And also when he gives instructions to husbands and wives:

"For this reason a man will leave his father and mother and be joined to his wife, and the two will become one flesh." This is a great mystery, and I am applying it to Christ and the church. (Eph. 5:31–32 NRSV)

Regarding these passages, William May and John Harvey observe that "the symbolic meaning of the sexual union of husband and wife is explicitly related to the meaning of Christ's union with His Church, and surely this has something to tell us of the meaning of our sexuality and of the male-female relationship."[16] Jesus, followed by Paul, appeals to Genesis for the divinely established norm. Marriage, then, belongs to the order of creation, which was declared by God to be "very good" (Gen. 1:31).

The sexual act within marriage—defined as the union of a man and a woman—is designed to mirror the covenantal union between God and humanity. Acts of marital infidelity destroy the analogy of God's faithfulness, which is intended to be reflected in the marriage bond. Fornication is forbidden because it constitutes repudiation of the order of creation, which finds its true reflection only in monogamous marriage.

When we apply this theological motif to the issue of homosexuality, we find that such practices are equally as incompatible with the marriage covenant as are other immoral practices. Revisionists attempt to avoid this judgment by suggesting that "homosexual marriage" might also reflect the covenantal union between God and humankind. However, as John Noonan writes, "homosexual marriage" fails on every point of the analogy: "Even more emphatic are the basic paradigms. The God of Israel is a faithful husband, He is never seen as a devoted homosexual lover. The Christ of the New Testament is a bridegroom, the Church is His bride; the couple are never presented as a homosexual pair. Human marriage itself, presented as the sign of Christ's union with the Church, is presented as the union of man and wife."[17]

These biblical themes present us with relationships that describe theological truths, each of which depends upon the sexual differentiation of male and female. The rejection of such distinctions would result in the distortion of the corresponding spiritual truth, as Noonan remarks, "In each instance there would have been something incongruous, ludicrous, even unthinkable in the choice of homosexual relations to signify deep, faithful, complementary love."[18]

CHAPTER 7

Homosexuality in Christian Tradition

I N TWO INFLUENTIAL BOOKS the late Yale professor John Boswell attempted to prove that homosexuality was tolerated for much of church history. Gay activists consider Boswell's work to be the definitive work on homosexuality and the church. They refer to Boswell's work as "proof" that opposition to homosexuality in the Church only arose in the late Middle Ages. In the words of Richard John Neuhaus, Boswell's *Christianity, Social Tolerance, and Homosexuality* "has become a kind of sacred text for those who want to morally legitimate the homosexual lifestyle."[1] An example of this attitude is homosexual psychiatrist Ralph Blair's triumphal warning: "Though some evangelicals may foolishly disregard as irrelevant the careful research Boswell has done with regard to 'tradition,' they cannot be so cavalier when it comes to what he has done with the biblical material."[2]

The openly homosexual Boswell, who died of AIDS in 1994, argues that after the dissolution of the Roman Empire there was a tolerant attitude toward homosexuality in the early Middle Ages. According to Boswell, the civil, ecclesiastical, and clerical pronouncements of the era against homosexual behavior did not reflect the views of the majority of Christians.

Boswell claims that in the tenth century a distinct homosexual subculture emerged that was tolerated by the institutional church. He further states that the alleged "gay subculture" in the church flourished until the early thirteenth century, when theological uniformity came to be viewed as more important than diversity and individual autonomy. This, along with the "natural law" theory propounded by Thomas Aquinas, which sought to establish a rational basis for Christian truth, led to the formal ecclesiastical condemnation of homosexual behavior.

Boswell concludes that theological opposition to homosexuality was a reflection of growing public intolerance in the late Middle Ages, an intolerance which persists to the present time.

It did not take long, after the initial blush of scholarly infatuation with Boswell's novel theory, for scholars to perceive the glaring weaknesses of *Christianity, Social Tolerance, and Homosexuality.* As Neuhaus notes, "The scholarly judgment of his book has ranged from the sharply critical to the dismissive to the devastating."[3]

Central to Boswell's argument is his insistence that "any distinction between 'friendship' and 'love' is arbitrary." Writing in *Communio,* Glenn W. Olsen finds Boswell's refusal to distinguish between the bond of friendship and entering into a sexual relationship to be a source of "hopeless confusion," with the result that "the whole task Boswell sets himself is impossible."[4]

With regard to Boswell's rejection of the traditional interpretation of the Sodom story, Olsen states, "To reject the most obvious progression of thought as 'purely imaginary' for no stated reason shows the special pleading that mars this book."[5] Olsen then describes Boswell's "thoroughly unsatisfactory discussion" of the New Testament evidence, which he characterizes as "a misguided attempt to defend the proposition" that the texts in question do not condemn homosexuality.[6]

Since in his book Boswell summarily disposes of the biblical arguments against homosexuality and contends that the church was indifferent to homosexual behavior, the reader is left to wonder why opposition to homosexuality arose in the Church. Even those taken with the book, such as John C. Moore of Hofstra University, who speaks of "the richness of this provocative book," recognizes this weakness. "[Boswell] has no explanation for the dramatic shift of the thirteenth century," writes Moore, "apart from saying that the origin of the change was more popular than clerical and that the new hostility was not caused by the Christian Bible, which had been there all along."[7]

In *Same-Sex Unions in Premodern Europe*, Boswell further elaborates his claim that the medieval Christian church tolerated homosexual behavior.[8] He claims historical precedent for same-sex union ceremonies within the church. At the heart of Boswell's argument are ancient church documents that describe a ritual practiced during antiquity and the High Middle Ages in the eastern Mediterranean. The ritual described in these liturgical documents is called *adelphopoiesis* (Greek, translated "the creation of a brother"). Boswell interprets this ritual as a ceremony for the blessing of a homosexual union.

Boswell's arguments, however, are fraught with misrepresentations and errors, including the following.

Boswell blatantly mistranslates the name of the ceremony of symbolic brotherhood. The spiritual union ceremony should not be translated "Office for Same-Sex Union," as Boswell suggests, thus falsely implying that homosexual unions enjoyed a legitimate status in the medieval church. In Greek the name of the ritual (*adelphopoiesis*) literally means "the creation of a brother." There is no suggestion of homosexuality in the Greek term.

The ceremony of symbolic brotherhood did not signify marital union. Brent Shaw notes that, as it does today, marriage in the Middle Ages meant "the formation of a common household, the sharing of everything in a permanent co-residential unit, [and] the formation of a family unit wherein the two partners were committed, ideally, to each other, with the intent to raise children."[9]

Boswell's so-called same-sex unions of this period, however, lack any of these important aspects of marriage. Consequently, as Shaw notes, "There is no indication in the texts themselves that these [rituals] are marriages in any sense."[10]

The ceremony of symbolic brotherhood represented spiritual union. A text taken from an eleventh-century Greek manuscript specifically states that the two parties are "joined together not by the bond of nature but by faith and in the mode of the spirit, granting unto them peace and love and oneness of mind." According to Robin Darling Young, associate professor of theology at the Catholic University of America, "The language employed in these texts does not suggest any kind of sexual connection between the two parties united in this particular bond."[11]

Boswell wrongly presumes that references to "love" indicate physical love. The Greek word *agape* is used in medieval recitations such as "Grant unto them unashamed fidelity and sincere love." Boswell assumes a direct sexual inference in such passages even though in the context *agape* lacks any such connotation. Shaw notes that while *agape* was occasionally used by Greek writers to refer to physical love, "such usages are extremely rare." Shaw continues,"But that is hardly the point. What remains indisputable is the significance of the word in ecclesiastical, theological, and liturgical writings—in the specific genres of Boswell's 'same-sex union' documents."[12]

From its inception the church has condemned homosexuality. Boswell claims that it was only "during the High Middle Ages" that the church prohibited homosexual behavior and began emphasizing the centrality of the biological family to society. This claim is patently false. Boswell ignores the teaching regarding the normative status of the traditional family structure that finds wide attestation among the early church fathers (see below). Furthermore, as Robin Young notes, the "early Byzantine law codes contain extremely harsh punishments for homosexual intercourse."[13]

In short, Boswell's supposed historical precedents for "homosexual marriages" within the church are fictitious. Since its inception, the Christian church has consistently prohibited homosexual behavior as one of many sinful deviations from monogamous marriage—a norm that dates back to Eden. Even revisionists such as Roger Shinn admit that, contra Boswell, homosexuality has consistently and unambiguously been condemned throughout church history: "The Christian tradition over the centuries has affirmed the heterosexual, monogamous, faithful marital union as normative for the divinely given meaning of the intimate sexual relationship."[14]

Homosexuality in Writings of the Early Church

The prohibition of all extramarital sexual relations—including homosexuality—is found in the earliest noncanonical Christian writings. Both the *Didache* and the *Epistle of Barnabas,* dating from the second century, include homosexuality among a list of sexual sins.[15] One of the first theologians of the church, Clement of Alexandria (died in A.D. 220) wrote that the Sodomites had "through much luxury fallen into uncleanness, practicing adultery shamelessly, and burning with insane love for boys."[16]

St. Basil (died in A.D. 379), a contemporary of Chrysostum, counseled young men to flee "intimate association," reminding such that "the enemy has indeed set many aflame through such means."[17] Basil recommended the same punishment for homosexual offences as for adultery, which was exclusion from the sacraments for fifteen years. St. Gregory of Nyssa (died in A.D. 398) also recommended this punishment and viewed homosexuality as unlawful pleasure.[18]

In his day St. John Chrysostum (died in A.D. 407) strongly opposed the practice of homosexuality, which he viewed as contrary to nature: "Blurring the natural order, men play the part of women, and women play the part of men, contrary to nature. . . . No passage is closed against evil lusts; and their sexuality is a public institution—they are roommates with indulgence."[19] As a result of their sin, writes Clement, "so did God bring upon them such a punishment as made the womb of the land for ever [sic] barren and destitute of all fruits."[20]

The conviction that homosexual acts are objectively wrong is continued by St. Augustine (died in A.D. 430), who wrote that "those crimes which are against nature must everywhere and always be detested and punished. The crimes of the men of Sodom are of this kind."[21]

Also in the fourth century, the *Theodosian Code* mandated "exquisite punishment" for those who would presume to enter into homosexual unions. By A.D. 390 the *Code* states that those who practice the "shameful custom of condemning a man's body, acting the part of a woman's" are to be burned at the stake.[22]

Emperor Justinian strengthened this legal tradition in the sixth century in the *Corpus Juris Civilis,* which became the foundation for Byzantine and later Western laws regulating sexual behavior. In the *Institutes* of the *Corpus* homosexuality is classed with adultery as punishable by death.[23] Justinian also issued two edicts that condemn such practices as "diabolical" and "the most disgraceful lusts."[24] From this time on, the prohibition of homosexual behavior became fixed in Western legal tradition.

Thomas Aquinas (died in A.D. 1274) discusses the subject of homosexuality in his *Summa Theologica* under the category of lust. Aquinas concludes that "since by the unnatural vices man transgresses that which has been determined by nature with regard to the use of venereal actions, it follows that in this matter this sin is gravest of all."[25]

The Protestant Reformers agreed with this judgment concerning homosexuality, as is indicated by Martin Luther's

(1483–1546) comment regarding the moral corruption he witnessed: "In Rome I myself saw some cardinals who were esteemed highly as saints because they were content to associate with women."[26] Similarly John Calvin (1509–64) refers to the sin of homosexuality as "the most serious of all, viz. that unnatural and filthy thing which was far too common in Greece."[27]

Various confessional statements since the Reformation reaffirm the rejection of homosexual behavior as contrary to the divine will for mankind.[28] Karl Barth briefly mentions homosexuality in his *Church Dogmatics,* referring to such behavior as a violation of God's created order. In a statement that reflects the common view of all major Christian denominations until the latter half of the twentieth century, Barth concludes that "the decisive word of Christian ethics must consist of a warning against entering upon the whole way of life which can only end in the tragedy of concrete homosexuality."[29]

Conclusion

J. D. Unwin, in his classic study *Sexual Regulations and Cultural Behavior,* examined the sexual mores of nearly one hundred civilizations over a period of several millennia.[30] Unwin began his studies with the self-confessed intent to "dispel the idea" that the limitation of "sexual impulses" is beneficial to society. The evidence, however, forced him to conclude that "expansive energy" (in such things as exploration and commerce) is displayed by the society only when sexuality is expressed within the boundaries of "absolute monogamy."[31] Unwin found that cultural vitality is directly related to a society's adherence to the biblical principle of heterosexual monogamy. As societies departed from the Judeo-Christian sexual ethic in favor of some form of "modified monogamy" or polygamy, their cultural energy diminished.[32]

Unwin's research confirms that the Judeo-Christian sexual ethic, rooted in the Bible as well as in nearly two thousand years of church teaching, has been a fundamental source of societal stability. Contrary to the claims of revisionists, the historical Christian opposition to homosexual behavior is integral to that ethic. On every level—the exegetical, historical, and theological—revisionists have failed to establish their contention that homosexuality is compatible with Christian faith. To the contrary, Muehl concludes that "efforts to redefine homosexual relationships as consistent with the biblical faith constitute an attack upon the very foundations of that faith."[33]

The revisionist methodology—with its inadequate account of the biblical witness, its denial of the continuing relevance of the moral law, and its subjective criteria for ethical evaluation—must be strenuously refuted in the name of authentic Christian morality.

CHAPTER 8

The Negative Health Effects of Homosexuality

THE ALEC I KNEW WAS at the peak of fitness. He was the enviable type who seemed to effortlessly maintain a youthful physique. On one occasion we happened to be discussing growing old. Alec turned to me and stated, with determination in his eyes and passion in his voice, that he had no intention of growing old, insisting, "I want to be able to get up in the morning and jog five miles!"

The gay lifestyle is obsessed with physical appearance because the social life of many homosexuals is closely tied to their sexual attractiveness. Unlike married couples who grow old together and whose value and commitment is not dependent upon physical attractiveness, older homosexuals typically experience harsh rejection by their youthful peers. No longer welcome at the party scene, they are shunned by younger gays. In contrast with married couples, who look forward to enduring love and respect from each other and from their children, the gay lifestyle is one of diminishing returns. Every year that passes means fewer opportunities for the fleeting sexual encounters that characterize the social lives of many homosexuals.

Hollywood and the media relentlessly propagate the image of fit, healthy, and well-adjusted homosexuals who are presumed to be the equivalent in every way to their heterosexual counterparts. However, the reality of the gay lifestyle is not consistent with this caricature, as recently conceded by the homosexual newspaper *New York Blade News:* "Reports at a national conference about sexually transmitted diseases indicate that gay men are in the highest risk group for several of the most serious diseases. . . . Scientists believe that the increased number of STD cases is the result of an increase in risky sexual practices by a growing number of gay men who believe HIV is no longer a life-threatening illness."[1]

Homosexual relationships are typically characterized by instability and promiscuity—two factors that greatly increase the incidence of serious and incurable sexually transmitted diseases. In addition, the gay lifestyle is characterized by unnatural, unhealthy, and dangerous sexual practices that contribute to disease. The following is a catalog of diseases that are endemic to the gay community.

Human Papillomavirus (HPV)

HPV is a collection of more than seventy types of viruses that can cause warts, or papillomas, on various parts of the body. More than twenty types of HPV are incurable STDs that can infect the genital tract of both men and women. Most HPV infections are asymptomatic, with only one in one hundred people experiencing genital warts. According to the homosexual newspaper, the *Washington Blade,* "A San Francisco study of gay and bisexual men revealed that HPV infection was almost universal among HIV-positive men, and that 60 percent of HIV-negative men carried HPV."[2]

HPV can lead to anal cancer. At the recent Fourth International AIDS Malignancy Conference at the National Institutes of Health, Dr. Andrew Grulich announced that "most instances of anal cancer are caused by a cancer-causing strain of human papillomavirus through receptive anal intercourse. HPV infects over 90 percent of HIV-positive gay men and 65 percent of HIV-negative gay men, according to a number of recent studies."[3]

Hepatitis

Gay men are at increased risk for contracting hepatitis—a potentially fatal liver disease that increases the risk of liver cancer. The three types of hepatitis are A, B, and C.

Hepatitis A and B are serious diseases caused by viruses that attack the liver. According to the Centers for Disease Control and Prevention (CDC), "outbreaks of hepatitis A among men who have sex with men are a recurring problem in many large cities in the industrialized world."[4]

Hepatitis B can cause lifelong infection, cirrhosis (scarring) of the liver, liver cancer, liver failure, and death. Each year in the United States, more than 80,000 people contract hepatitis B and nearly 5,000 die. The CDC reports that men who have sex with men are at increased risk for hepatitis B.[5]

Hepatitis C is an inflammation of the liver that can cause cirrhosis, liver failure and liver cancer. The virus can lie dormant in the body for up to thirty years before flaring up. Although less so than with hepatitis A and B, men who have sex with men while engaging in unsafe sexual practices remain at increased risk for contracting hepatitis C.[6]

Gonorrhea

Gonorrhea is an inflammatory disease that traditionally occurs on the genitals. The increase of gonorrhea infections appearing in the rectal region and in the throat is tied to sexual practices common among gay men. Although treatable with antibiotics, the CDC reports that only "about 50 percent of men have some signs or symptoms," and "many women who are infected have no symptoms of infection."[7] Untreated gonorrhea can have serious and permanent health consequences, including infertility and damage to the prostate and urethra.

The CDC released data showing that male rectal gonorrhea is increasing among homosexuals amidst an overall decline in national gonorrhea rates. The report attributed the increase to a larger percentage of homosexuals engaging in unsafe sexual behavior.[8]

The incidence of throat gonorrhea is strongly associated with homosexual behavior. The *Canadian Medical Association Journal* found that "gonorrhea was associated with urethral discharge . . . and homosexuality (3.7 times higher than the rate among heterosexuals)."[9] Similarly, a study in the *Journal of Clinical Pathology* found that homosexual men had a much higher prevalence of pharyngeal (throat) gonorrhea—15.2 percent compared with 4.1 percent for heterosexual men.[10]

Syphilis

Syphilis is a venereal disease that, if left untreated, can spread throughout the body over time, causing serious heart abnormalities, mental disorders, blindness, and death. The initial symptoms of syphilis are often mild and painless, leading some individuals to avoid seeking treatment. According to the National Institutes of Health, the disease may be mistaken for other common illnesses: "Syphilis has sometimes been called 'the great imitator' because its early symptoms are similar to those of many other diseases." Early symptoms include rashes, moist warts in the groin area, slimy white patches in the mouth, or pus-filled bumps resembling chicken pox.[11] According to the *Archives of Internal Medicine,* homosexuals acquire syphilis at a rate ten times that of heterosexuals.[12]

In addition, the CDC reports that those who contract syphilis face potentially deadly health consequences: "It is now known that the genital sores caused by syphilis in adults also make it easier to transmit and acquire HIV infection sexually. There is a two- to fivefold increased risk of acquiring HIV infection when syphilis is present."[13]

Gay Bowel Syndrome

The diseases that afflicted Alec at the end of his futile battle with AIDS came from gay bowel syndrome (GBS).[14] The *Journal of the American Medical Association* refers to GBS problems such as proctitis, proctocolitis, and enteritis as "sexually transmitted gastrointestinal syndromes."[15] Many of the bacterial and protozoa pathogens that cause GBS are found in feces and transmitted to the digestive system. According to the prohomosexual text *Anal Pleasure and Health,* "Sexual activities provide many opportunities for tiny amounts of contaminated feces to find their way into the mouth of a sexual partner. . . . The most direct route is oral-anal contact."[16]

Proctitis and proctocolitis are inflammations of the rectum and colon that cause pain, bloody rectal discharge and rectal spasms. Proctitis is associated with STDs such as gonorrhea, chlamydia, herpes, and syphilis that are widespread among homosexuals.[17] The Sexually Transmitted Disease Information Center of the *Journal of the American Medical Association* reports that "[p]roctitis occurs predominantly among persons who participate in anal intercourse."

Enteritis is inflammation of the small intestine. According to the Sexually Transmitted Disease Information Center of the *Journal of the American Medical Association,* "Enteritis occurs among those whose sexual practices include oral-fecal contact."[18] Enteritis can cause abdominal pain, severe cramping, intense diarrhea, fever, malabsorption of nutrients, and weight loss.[19] According to *The Health Implications of Homosexuality* by the

Medical Institute for Sexual Health, some pathogens associated with enteritis and proctocolitis (see below) "appear only to be sexually transmitted among men who have sex with men."[20]

HIV/AIDS among Homosexuals

The human immunodeficiency virus (HIV) is responsible for causing AIDS, for which there is no cure. The CDC reports that "men who have sex with men" (MSM) comprise the single largest exposure category of people with AIDS in the United States. "Men who have sex with men" and "men who have sex with men and inject drugs" account for about two-thirds of the cumulative total of male AIDS cases.[21]

Homosexuals with HIV are at increased risk for developing other life-threatening diseases. A paper delivered at the Fourth International AIDS Malignancy Conference at the National Institutes of Health reported that homosexual men with HIV have "a 37-fold increase in anal cancer, a 4-fold increase in Hodgkin's disease (cancer of the lymph nodes), a 2.7-fold increase in cancer of the testicles, and a 2.5-fold increase in lip cancer."[22]

Failing to Disclose HIV Status to Sex Partners

A study presented at the XIII International AIDS Conference in Durban, South Africa, disclosed that a significant number of homosexual and bisexual men with HIV "continue to engage in unprotected sex with people who have no idea they could be contracting HIV."[23] Researchers from the University of California, San Francisco, found that 36 percent of homosexuals engaging in unprotected oral, anal, or vaginal sex failed to disclose that they were HIV positive to casual sex partners.[24]

A CDC report revealed that, in 1997, 45 percent of homosexuals who had unprotected anal intercourse during the previous six months did not know the HIV status of all their sex partners. Even more alarming, among those who had unprotected anal intercourse *and multiple partners,* 68 percent did not know the HIV status of their partners.[25]

Young Homosexuals Are at Increased Risk

Following in the footsteps of the generation of homosexuals decimated by AIDS, younger homosexuals are engaging in dangerous sexual practices at an alarming rate.

HIV incidence is on the rise among teens and young adults. The CDC reports that "even though AIDS incidence (the number of new cases diagnosed during a given time period, usually a year) is declining, *there has not been a comparable decline in the number of newly diagnosed HIV cases among youth.*"[26] Young homosexual men are at particular risk. The CDC estimates that "at least half of all new HIV infections in the United States are among people under twenty-five, and the majority of young people are infected sexually."[27]

Homosexuals with STDs Are at Greatly Increased Risk for HIV Infection

Studies of homosexuals treated in STD clinics show high rates of HIV infection.[28] A CDC study attributed the high infection rate to having high numbers of anonymous sex partners: "Syphilis, gonorrhea, and chlamydia apparently have been introduced into a population of MSM who have large numbers of anonymous partners, which can result in rapid and extensive transmission of STDs."[29] The CDC report concluded, "Persons with STDs, including genital ulcer disease and nonulcerative STD, have a twofold to fivefold increased risk for HIV infection."[30]

Anal Cancer

Homosexuals are at increased risk for this rare type of cancer, which is potentially fatal if the anal-rectal tumors metastasize to other bodily organs. Dr. Joel Palefsky, a leading expert in the field of anal cancer, reports that while the incidence of anal cancer in the United States is only about one person per 100,000, that number soars to thirty-five people per 100,000 for homosexuals. That rate doubles again for those who are HIV positive, which, according to Palefsky, is "roughly ten times higher than the current rate of cervical cancer."[31] Also, at the Fourth International AIDS Malignancy Conference at the National Institutes of Health in May 2000, Dr. Andrew Grulich announced that the incidence of anal cancer among homosexuals with HIV "was raised thirty-seven-fold compared with the general population."[32]

Lesbians Are at Risk for Contracting STDs

Many lesbians have had sex with men, putting them at risk for contracting STDs. The *Washington Blade,* citing a 1998 study in the *Journal of Infectious Diseases,* reported that "the study's data confirmed previous scientific observations that most women who have sex with women also have had sex with men." The study added that "sex with men in the prior year was common, as were sexual practices between female partners that possibly could transmit HPV."[33]

Lesbians have more male sex partners than their heterosexual counterparts. A study of sexually transmitted disease among lesbians reviewed in the *Washington Blade* notes, "Behavioral research also demonstrates that a woman's sexual identity is not an accurate predictor of behavior, with a large proportion of 'lesbian' women reporting sex with (often high-risk) men."[34] The study found that "the median number of lifetime male sexual partners was significantly greater for WSW (women who have sex with women) than controls (twelve partners versus six). WSW were significantly more likely to report more than fifty lifetime male sexual partners."[35]

A study in the *American Journal of Public Health* concurs that bisexual women are at increased risk for contracting sexually transmitted diseases: "Our findings corroborate the finding that WSMW (women who have sex with men and women) are more likely than WSMO (women who have sex with men only) to engage in various high-risk behaviors" and also "to engage in a greater number of risk-related behaviors." The study suggested that the willingness to engage in risky sexual practices "could be tied to a pattern of sensation-seeking behavior."[36]

Homosexuals are also responsible for spreading HIV to women. A five-year study by the CDC of 3,492 homosexuals aged fifteen to twenty-two found that one in six also had sex with women. Of those having sex with women, one-fourth "said they recently had unprotected sex with both men and women." Nearly 7 percent of the men in the study were HIV positive. "The study confirms that young bisexual men are a 'bridge' for HIV transmission to women."[37]

"Exclusive" Lesbian Relationships Also at Risk

The assumption that lesbians involved in exclusive sexual relationships are at reduced risk for sexual disease is false. The journal *Sexually Transmitted Infections* concludes, "The risk behavior profile of exclusive WSW was similar to all WSW." One reason for this is because lesbians "were significantly more likely to report past sexual contact with a homosexual or bisexual man and sexual contact with an IDU (intravenous drug user)."[38]

Cancer Risk Factors for Lesbians

Citing a 1999 report released by the Institute of Medicine, an arm of the National Academy of Sciences, the *Washington Blade* notes that "various studies on lesbian health suggest that certain cancer risk factors occur with greater frequency in this population. These factors include higher rates of smoking, alcohol use, poor diet, and being overweight."[39] Elsewhere the *Blade* also reports, "Some experts believe lesbians might be more likely than women in general to develop breast or cervical cancer because a disproportionate number of them fall into high-risk categories."[40]

STDs among Lesbians

A study of the medical records of 1,408 lesbians in *Sexually Transmitted Infections* found that WSW are at a significantly higher risk for certain STDs: "We demonstrated a higher prevalence of BV (bacterial vaginosis), hepatitis C, and HIV risk behaviors in WSW as compared with controls."[41]

Compulsive Behavior among Lesbians

A study published in *Nursing Research* found that lesbians are three times more likely to abuse alcohol and to suffer from other compulsive behaviors: "Like most problem drinkers, thirty-two (91 percent) of the participants had abused other drugs as well as alcohol, and many reported compulsive difficulties with food (34 percent), codependency (29 percent), sex (11 percent), and money (6 percent)." In addition, "Forty-six percent had been heavy drinkers with frequent drunkenness."[42]

Alcohol Abuse among Homosexuals and Lesbians

The *Journal of Consulting and Clinical Psychologists* reports that lesbian women consume alcohol more frequently and in larger amounts than heterosexual women. Lesbians were at significantly greater risk than heterosexual women for both binge drinking (19.4 percent compared to 11.7 percent) and for heavy drinking (7 percent compared to 2.7 percent).[43]

Although the *Journal of Consulting and Clinical Psychologists* article found no significant connection between male homosexuals and alcohol abuse, a study in *Family Planning Perspectives* concluded that male homosexuals were at greatly increased risk for alcoholism: "Among men, by far the most important risk group consisted of homosexual and bisexual men, who were more than nine times as likely as heterosexual men to have a history of problem drinking." The study noted that problem drinking may contribute to the "significantly higher STD rates among gay and bisexual men."[44]

Violence in Lesbian and Homosexual Relationships

A study in the *Journal of Interpersonal Violence* examined conflict and violence in lesbian relationships. The researchers found that 90 percent of the lesbians surveyed had been recipients of one or more acts of verbal abuse from their intimate partners during the year prior to this study, with 31 percent reporting one or more incidents of physical abuse.[45]

Another survey of 1,099 lesbians in the *Journal of Social Service Research* found that "slightly more than half of the [lesbians] reported that they had been abused by a female lover/partner. The most frequently indicated forms of abuse were verbal/emotional/psychological abuse and combined physical-psychological abuse."[46]

In their book *Men Who Beat the Men Who Love Them: Battered Gay Men and Domestic Violence,* D. Island and P. Letellier report that "the incidence of domestic violence among gay men is nearly double that in the heterosexual population."[47]

The Low Rate of Violence within Marriage

Homosexual and lesbian relationships are far more violent than traditional married households. The Bureau of Justice Statistics reports that married women in traditional families experience the lowest rate of violence compared with women in other types of relationships.[48]

A report by the Medical Institute for Sexual Health concurs and points out a significant flaw in many studies of violence in relationships: "It should be noted that most studies of family violence do not differentiate between married and unmarried partner status. Studies that do make these distinctions have found that marriage relationships tend to have the least intimate-partner violence when compared to cohabiting or dating relationships."[49]

High Incidence of Mental Health Problems among Homosexuals and Lesbians

A national survey of lesbians published in the *Journal of Consulting and Clinical Psychology* found that 75 percent of the nearly two thousand respondents had pursued psychological counseling of some kind—many for treatment of long-term depression or sadness.

> Among the sample as a whole, there was a distressingly high prevalence of life events and behaviors related to mental health problems. Thirty-seven percent had been physically abused and 32 percent had been raped or sexually attacked. Nineteen percent had been involved in incestuous relationships while growing up. Almost one-third used tobacco on a daily basis and about 30 percent drank alcohol more than once a week; 6 percent drank daily. One in five smoked marijuana more than once a month. Twenty-one percent of the sample had thoughts about suicide sometimes or often and 18 percent had actually tried to kill themselves. . . . More than half had felt too nervous to accomplish ordinary activities at some time during the past year and over one-third had been depressed.[50]

Greater Risk for Suicide

A study of twins that examined the relationship between homosexuality and suicide, published in the *Archives of General Psychiatry,* found that homosexuals with same-sex partners were at greater risk for overall mental health problems and were 6.5 times more likely than their twins to have attempted suicide. The higher rate was not attributable to mental health or substance abuse disorders.[51]

Another study published simultaneously in *Archives of General Psychiatry* followed 1,007 individuals from birth. Those classified as gay, lesbian, or bisexual were significantly more likely to have had mental health problems.[52] Significantly, in his comments on the studies in the same issue of the journal, D. Bailey cautioned against various speculative explanations of the results, such as the view that "widespread prejudice against homosexual people causes them to be unhappy or worse, mentally ill."[53]

Reduced Life Span

A study published in the *International Journal of Epidemiology* on the mortality rates of homosexuals concluded that they have a significantly reduced life expectancy: "In a major Canadian centre, life expectancy at age twenty for gay and bisexual men is eight to twenty years less than for all men. If the same pattern of mortality were to continue, we estimate that nearly half of gay and bisexual men currently aged twenty years will not reach their sixty-fifth birthday. Under even the most liberal assumptions, gay and bisexual men in this urban centre are now experiencing a life expectancy similar to that experienced by all men in Canada in the year 1871."[54]

In 1995, long after the deadly effects of AIDS and other STDs became widely known, homosexual author Urvashi Vaid expressed one of the goals of her fellow activists: "We have an agenda to create a society in which homosexuality is regarded as healthy, natural, and normal. To me that is the most important agenda item."[55] Debilitating illness, chronic disease, psychological problems, and early death suffered by homosexuals is the legacy of this tragically misguided activism, which puts the furthering of an "agenda" above saving the lives of those whose interests they purport to represent.

CHAPTER 9

Gay Households

O N MY LAST TRIP TO Minneapolis (before the dinner when he revealed his intentions) I visited Alec at his imposing office. As we sat and talked he said, "You know, Tim, you've been on my mind a lot these days." He fidgeted with his desk drawer. "I bought a card that expressed my feelings—but I didn't know whether to send it to you."

I sat across from Alec, watching him decide whether to retrieve the card from the drawer. What was this card that he hesitated to give to me? It was obviously more than a humorous friendship card. I was intuitively glad he didn't send it—and that in the end he decided against opening the drawer to give it to me.

Later I realized what was going on. Alec's emotional dynamics paralleled those of normal heterosexual romance. He was exhibiting the characteristics of an infatuated young man who hopes a certain young lady will return his affection. Not knowing what her reaction will be, he hesitates to share his feelings. He purchases a token of his affection to speak for his feelings. But fearing rejection, he holds back and does not give it to her. When he has opportunity he makes fleeting physical contact—a touch of the hand, a brush of her cheek—hoping that it will stir emotions within her.

But the analogy is desperately flawed. Although the homosexual may experience many of the same romantic emotions shared between a man and a woman, the two can never be equivalent. This is because "normal" love—normal in the sense of biological design and moral dictates and religious belief—is intended to culminate in marriage, family, and children. United together, a man and a woman build the "family tree," thereby enlarging personal, biological roots and contributing to the building of society. By its very nature, homosexual "love" cannot accomplish these personal or societal goals.

On a personal level, as we shall see, male homosexuals exhibit compulsive sexual behavior, ever seeking further conquests without the tempering provided by the feminine emphasis upon commitment and the nurturing of children. Lesbian "couples" fare little better, as indicated by the negative health implications of that lifestyle. As a result, homosexual relationships are transient, rarely achieving any degree of stability and fidelity.

Homosexual apologists are keenly aware that the gay lifestyle is inherently promiscuous. Yet they choose to blame such profligate behavior on society itself—more specifically, what they consider to be an archaic, repressive Judeo-Christian morality.

The argument goes as follows: homosexual promiscuity is the direct result of societal oppression. Gays and lesbians have been forced to live their lives in the closet, which has led to the kinds of excesses associated with their community. If only society would recognize and grant legitimacy to gay relationships, then gays and lesbians would have the necessary support to live "normal" lives. Most important, if gays and lesbians were permitted to marry, then they would have the necessary societal support with which to settle down and live faithful, monogamous lives just like married people.

The evidence, however, does not support this claim. Surveys indicate a growing acceptance of gays and lesbians over the past few decades. If the above argument were true, we should be seeing an accompanying decline in promiscuity and sexually transmitted diseases in the gay community. Yet we are seeing the opposite.

Homosexuals continue to have shockingly high numbers of sexual partners and to engage in risky sexual practices. There is no evidence that societal acceptance will "tame" the homosexual lifestyle: if anything, increasing acceptance leads to ever more "in-your-face" flaunting of the more sordid sexual practices that remained hidden "in the closet" when society was less tolerant of homosexuality.

Moreover, there is little evidence that homosexuals as a whole desire to "settle down" to conventional marriage. Gay activists have made it abundantly clear that they have no intention of imitating the restrictive morality of "breeders," their contemptuous designation for parents.

Romance between a man and a woman naturally blossoms into marriage, children, and the building of society. That is God's wonderful and fulfilling design for human sexuality. Homosexual infatuation can accomplish none of those goals, but can only culminate in hollow, unnatural lust. Hence the relentless drive for the next "conquest" in a vain attempt to find meaning in the sexual act.

I have no idea how many such relationships possessed Alec during his lifetime. I suspect that each followed the same predictable trajectory: a season of intense attraction that typically included a sexual relationship. After the sexual conquest, it was only a matter of time before interest would begin to wane. Eventually another young man would catch Alec's eye. More often than not there would be the usual bitterness and recrimination on the part of the newly abandoned. The cycle would repeat itself again and again, until as with so many others, Alec's life was cut short by AIDS.

And I would venture that these fleeting amours failed to positively impact Alec's life, deepen him as a person, enrich his marriage, or strengthen his role as a father. On the contrary, they caused extraordinary damage to his marriage and family, resulted in disease and early death, and forever tainted an otherwise remarkable legacy.

But what about those gays and lesbians who insist they want to enter into "committed" homosexual relationships, settle down, and raise children? Let's take a look at why homosexual households are not the equivalent of marriage and why children should not be subjected to the dangers inherent in such environments.

Putting Children at Risk

It was just a few sentences buried in a long article in *USA Today* that attempted to portray homosexual parenting in a positive light, yet it spoke volumes. The *USA Today* article claimed that the "leading edge of scientific research" was uncovering some "distinctive qualities" of such households.[1] This odd choice of words was doubtlessly required by the fact that research claiming to be supportive of gay parenting is both inconclusive and controversial.

It was not the ambiguous research but the words of those living in homosexual households that told the real, heart-rending story of children who are intentionally deprived of either a mother or a father. The *USA Today* article quoted Yale University child psychiatrist Kyle Pruett: "We do know kids look for same-sex role models, and they benefit from having mothers and fathers." The article continues: "The 'looking' process starts very early. The three-year-old son of Jen Bleakley and Nina Jacobson of Los Angeles has asked his lesbian moms, 'Do I have a daddy?' That has progressed to 'I want a daddy' and 'Daddies are fun.'"

Similarly, the article quotes four-year-old Travis, born to a surrogate mother and adopted by Gregg Cartagine and his homosexual partner. What does little Travis think about being deprived of a mother? Cartagine admits, "Sometimes he'll call one of us Mommy, and occasionally we'll play peek-a-boo and he'll ask 'Where's Mommy?' so he's still working it out in his mind."

Little Travis will likely still be wondering why he does not have a mommy for many years to come. The *USA Today* article may treat these anecdotal stories in a lighthearted "kids say the darndest things" vein, but they represent the cry from the heart of children yearning for their "lost" parent.

Gay activists are keen to present the gay lifestyle as "just like" heterosexual marriages and insist that children should be entrusted to such households. They claim that gay couples have the capacity to be just as "committed" as married people—and would be even more committed if only society would legalize them.

However, as we shall see, even so-called committed gay relationships are seldom monogamous. Astoundingly, gay activists actually redefine the term *committed* to include sexual partners outside the relationship—an arrangement that few heterosexual spouses would consent to.

Despite the rapidly growing movement to legitimize gay marriage and gay adoption, the fact remains that only a miniscule number of households in the United States contain children being raised by homosexuals. The 2000 census reported 601,209 households containing same-sex partners out of a total of more than 105 million households.[2] Those figures indicate that only six in one thousand, or 0.57 percent of households are homosexual.

Only a small percentage of those households contain children. A survey in *Demography* reported 95 percent of partnered male homosexual and 78 percent of partnered lesbian households do *not* have children.[3] (Of course, some homosexuals who live alone are also attempting to raise children, adding the problems inherent in single parenthood to those resulting from their homosexuality.)

Despite the small number of such households, there has been no lack of scholarly interest in the subject of homosexual parenting, with many studies attempting to show that children raised in gay and lesbian households fare no worse than those reared in traditional families. The author of an article in one professional journal, for instance, wrote, "[T]he weight of evidence gathered . . . is persuasive in demonstrating that . . . there is no systematic difference between gay and nongay parents. . . . No data have pointed to any risk to children as a result of growing up in a family with one or more gay parents."[4]

However, much of that research fails to meet acceptable standards for psychological research; it is compromised by research flaws and driven by political agendas instead of an objective search for truth. The overlooking of such deficiencies in research papers on homosexual failures can be attributed to the "politically correct" determination within those in the social science professions to "prove" that homosexual households are no different than traditional families.

Problems with Homosexual Parenting Studies

A study published in the *Journal of Divorce and Remarriage* reviewed fourteen studies on homosexual parenting according to accepted scientific standards. The study found that "all of the studies lacked external validity. The conclusion that there are no significant differences in children raised by lesbian mothers versus heterosexual mothers is not supported by the published research data base."[5] Let's look at some of the limitations of these studies.

Inadequate Sample Size

Studies on homosexual parenting are weakened by small sample sizes. A report in *Developmental Psychology*, commenting on studies of the children of gay and lesbian parents, notes that "available studies [are] insufficiently large to generate much statistical power."[6]

Similarly, a study in the homosexual advocacy publication, the *Journal of Homosexuality*, admitted that "researchers must deal with many methodological problems in locating and testing gay fathers in numbers sufficiently large to make acceptable statistical analyses of data. For this reason, what is known currently about gay fathers is weakened by these methodological problems. It is practically impossible to obtain a representative sample of gay fathers."[7]

In her study of lesbian families, lesbian scholar-activist Charlotte Patterson acknowledges "some concerns relevant to sampling issues," in her own research. These include the fact that "most of the families who took part in the Bay Area Families Study were headed by lesbian mothers who were white, well-educated, relatively affluent, and living in the greater San Francisco Bay area. For these reasons, no claims about representativeness of the present sample can be made."[8] Unfortunately such admissions of limitations—which raise serious questions about the validity of the research itself—are often buried in the progay parenting fervor of the article.

By contrast, R. Green et al., writing in *Archives of Sexual Behavior*, found that the few experimental studies that included larger samples reported "developmentally important, statistically significant differences between children reared by homosexual parents compared to heterosexual parents. For example, children raised by homosexuals were found to have greater parental encouragement for cross-gender behavior [and] greater amounts of cross-dressing and cross-gender play/role behavior."[9]

Lack of Random Sampling

Researchers use random sampling to ensure that the study participants are representative of the population being studied (in this case, homosexuals or lesbians). Findings from unrepresentative samples have no legitimate generalization to the larger population.

Researchers Laura Lott-Whitehead and C. T. Tully admit the inherent weaknesses in their study of lesbian mothers: "This study was descriptive and, therefore, had inherent in its design methodological flaws consistent with other similar studies. Perhaps the most serious concerns representativeness. . . . Probability random sampling . . . was impossible. This study does not purport to contain a representative sample, and thus generalizability cannot be assumed."[10]

Similarly, Golombok et al. admit that their study used "volunteers obtained through gay and single-parent magazines and associations. Obviously these do not constitute random samples, and it is not possible to know what biases are involved in the method of sample selection."[11] We see in these examples once again that the results of prohomosexual parenting studies are admittedly compromised by the lack of adherence to basic research standards.

Lack of Anonymity of Research Participants

Research procedures guaranteeing complete anonymity are necessary to prevent a source of bias as to who will consent to participate as a research subject and to ensure the truthfulness and candor of their answers. Mary B. Harris and Pauline H. Turner point out in the *Journal of Homosexuality*, "Most gay/lesbian parents who participate in such research are concerned about their parenting and their children, and most have established a public gay identity. 'Closet' gay parents are difficult to identify, and their problems may be quite different from those of more openly gay parents."[12]

Study participants who are "open" homosexual parents are less likely to provide forthright answers about any negative effects of homosexual parenting because they have a public investment in "proving" that their lifestyle choice is a positive one.

Harris and Turner employed superior research techniques to ensure the complete anonymity of their research subjects. As a result, in contrast to other studies, they found problems associated with being a homosexual parent that had gone unreported in earlier studies: "Perhaps the anonymity of the present sampling procedure made subjects more willing to acknowledge those problems than those in earlier studies."[13]

Self-Presentation Bias

A lack of random sampling and the absence of controls guaranteeing anonymity allow subjects to present a misleading picture to the researcher. Such a picture often conforms to the subject's attitudes or opinions, suppressing evidence that does not suit the image the subject desires to present. In their National Lesbian Family Study, Nanette Gartrell et al. found that eighteen of nineteen studies of homosexual parents used a research procedure that was contaminated by self-presentation bias.

Gartrell mentions the methodological problems of one longitudinal study of lesbian families: "Some may have volunteered for this project because they were motivated to demonstrate that lesbians were capable of producing healthy, happy children. To the extent that these subjects might wish to present themselves and their families in the best possible light, the study findings may be shaped by self-justification and self-presentation bias."[14]

Problems with the Homosexual Lifestyle

In addition to the methodological considerations indicating that many studies of homosexual parenting are unreliable, a considerable body of evidence shows that the homosexual lifestyle is inconsistent with the proper raising of children. Homosexual relationships are characteristically unstable and are fundamentally incapable of providing children the security they need.

Homosexual Promiscuity

Studies indicate that the average male homosexual has hundreds of sex partners in his lifetime. It is difficult for even "committed" homosexual partners to part with this pattern of promiscuous behavior, which many homosexuals consider to be an integral part of the "gay lifestyle." A. P. Bell and M. S. Weinberg, in their classic study of male and female homosexuality, found that 43 percent of white male homosexuals had sex with five hundred or more partners, with 28 percent having 1,000 or more sex partners.[15]

A study of the sexual profiles of 2,583 older homosexuals published in the *Journal of Sex Research* reported similar high levels of promiscuity among gay men. The study found that "the modal range for number of sexual partners ever [of homosexuals] was 101–500." In addition, 10.2 percent to 15.7 percent had between 501 and 1000 partners. A further 10.2 percent to 15.7 percent reported having had more than 1000 lifetime sexual partners.[16] Such a lifestyle is manifestly not conducive to a healthy and wholesome atmosphere for the raising of children.

Promiscuity among Homosexual "Couples"

Even those homosexual relationships in which the partners consider themselves to be in a committed relationship, the meaning of *committed* typically means something radically different than in heterosexual marriage. In *The Male Couple,* authors David P. McWhirter and Andrew M. Mattison report that in a study of 156 males in homosexual relationships lasting from one to thirty-seven years, "Only seven couples have a totally exclusive sexual relationship, and these men all have been together for less than five years. Stated another way, all couples with a relationship lasting more than five years have incorporated some provision for outside sexual activity in their relationships."[17] Most of the males studied understood sexual relations outside the relationship to be the norm and viewed monogamy as oppressive.

Significant for the issue of stability in such households is the finding reported in *Male and Female Homosexuality.* Authors M. Saghir and E. Robins found that the average male homosexual live-in relationship lasts between two and three years.[18] To intentionally place children in households with a revolving bedroom door is unconscionable and will inevitably result in confusion, insecurity, and other emotional problems.

Comparison of Homosexual Couples and Heterosexual Spouses

Homosexual advocates counter, "Homosexual promiscuity is no different than that which exists within traditional marriage." However, the following statistics regarding sexual fidelity within marriage are revealing.

In *Sex in America,* called by the *New York Times* "the most important study of American sexual behavior since the Kinsey reports," Robert T. Michael et al. reported that 90 percent of wives and 75 percent of husbands claim never to have had extramarital sex.[19] Also, a nationally representative survey of 884 men and 1,288 women published in the *Journal of Sex Research* found that 77 percent of married men and 88 percent of married women had remained faithful to their marriage vows.[20]

While the rate of fidelity within marriage cited by these studies remains far from ideal, there is a magnum order of difference between the negligible lifetime fidelity rate cited for homosexuals and the 75 to 90 percent cited for married couples. This indicates that even "committed" homosexual relationships display a fundamental incapacity for the faithfulness and commitment that is axiomatic to the institution of marriage.

Sexual Identity Confusion

The above risk factors contribute to emotional difficulties suffered by many children raised in homosexual households. Growing evidence shows that children raised in homosexual households are more likely to engage in sexual experimentation and in homosexual behavior.

Studies indicate that 0.3 percent of adult females report having practiced homosexual behavior in the past year, 0.4 percent have practiced homosexual behavior in the last five years, and 3 percent have ever practiced homosexual behavior in their lifetime.[21] By contrast, a study in *Developmental Psychology* found that 12 percent of the children of lesbians became active lesbians themselves—at least four times the base rate of lesbianism in the adult female population.[22]

Numerous studies indicate that while nearly 5 percent of males report having had a homosexual experience sometime in their lives, the number of exclusive homosexuals is considerably less: between 1 and 2 percent of males report exclusive homosexual behavior over a several-year period.[23]

However, J. M. Bailey et al. found that 9 percent of the adult sons of homosexual fathers were homosexual in their adult sexual behavior: "The rate of homosexuality in the sons (9 percent) is several times higher than that suggested by the population-based surveys and is consistent with a degree of father-to-son transmission."[24]

In their study, Golombok and Tasker reported a clear connection between being raised in a lesbian family and homosexuality: "With respect to actual involvement in same-gender sexual relationships, there was a significant difference between groups. . . . None of the children from heterosexual families had experienced a lesbian or gay relationship." By contrast, five (29 percent) of the seventeen daughters and one (13 percent) of the eight sons in homosexual families reported having at least one same-sex relationship.[25]

These findings have most recently been confirmed in a study appearing in the *American Sociological Review.* Authors Judith Stacey and Timothy J. Biblarz alluded to the "political incorrectness" of their finding of higher rates of homosexuality among children raised in homosexual households: "We recognize the political dangers of pointing out that recent studies indicate that a higher proportion of children of lesbigay parents are themselves apt to engage in homosexual activity."

Stacy and Biblarz also reported that "adolescent and young adult girls raised by lesbian mothers appear to have been more sexually adventurous and less chaste. . . . In other words, once again, children (especially girls) raised by lesbians appear to depart from traditional gender-based norms, while children raised by heterosexual mothers appear to conform to them."[26]

Incest in Homosexual Parent Families

A study in *Adolescence* found that "a disproportionate percentage—29 percent—of the adult children of homosexual parents had been specifically subjected to sexual molestation by that homosexual parent, compared to only 0.6 percent of adult children of heterosexual parents having reported sexual relations with their parent. . . . Having a homosexual parent(s) appears to increase the risk of incest with a parent by a factor of about 50."[27]

Implications for Homosexual Parenting

Demands that homosexuals be accorded the right to marry and to adopt children advance the gay agenda by minimizing the differences between homosexual and heterosexual behavior to make homosexuality look as normal as possible. However, as already shown, only a small minority of gay and lesbian households have children. Beyond that, the evidence also indicates that comparatively few homosexuals choose to establish households together—the type of setting that is a prerequisite for the rearing of children.

Gay activists admit that the ultimate goal of the drive to legitimize homosexual marriage and adoption is to change the essential character of marriage, removing precisely the aspects of fidelity and chastity that promote stability in the home. They pursue their goal heedless of the fact that stable two-parent households are clearly preferable for the rearing of children.[28]

Paula Ettelbrick, former legal director of the Lambda Legal Defense and Education Fund, has stated, "Being queer is more than setting up house, sleeping with a person of the same gender, and seeking state approval for doing so. . . . Being queer means pushing the parameters of sex, sexuality, and family, and in the process transforming the very fabric of society."[29]

This view of marriage is widespread in the homosexual community. According to the *Mendola Report,* a mere 26 percent of homosexuals believe that commitment is most important in a marriage relationship.[30] Those who support the concept of homosexual "families" admit to their unsuitability for children, as reported by a study in *Family Relations:* "Even individuals who believe that same-sex relationships are a legitimate choice for adults may feel that children will suffer from being reared in such families."[31]

Prohomosexual researchers J. J. Bigner and R. B. Jacobson candidly describe the homosexual father as "socioculturally unique," trying to take on "two apparently opposing roles: that of a father (with all its usual connotations) and that of a homosexual man." They describe the homosexual father as "both structurally and psychologically at social odds with his interest in keeping one foot in both worlds: parenting and homosexuality."[32]

In truth, the two roles are fundamentally incompatible. The instability, susceptibility to disease, and domestic violence that is disproportionate in homosexual relationships would normally render such households unfit to be granted custody of children. However, in the current social imperative to grant legitimacy to the practice of homosexuality in every conceivable area of life, such considerations are often ignored.

Children are not guinea pigs to be used in social experiments to redefine the institutions of marriage and family. They are vulnerable individuals with vital emotional and developmental needs. The great harm done by denying them both a mother and a father in a committed marriage will not easily be reversed, and society will pay a grievous price for its ill-advised adventurism.

CHAPTER 10

Homosexuality and Child Sexual Abuse

YOU SHOULDN'T HAVE done it. It ruined our lives!" cried a boy from the back of an Ohio courtroom as he confronted the man who sexually molested him. The perpetrator, a former Boy Scout leader, had just pleaded guilty to rape and sexual battery. As yet another example of the cycle of sexual abuse, the pedophile claimed that he, too, had been sexually molested as a child.

Dave, another victim of sexual molestation by a Boy Scout leader, was reduced to living on the streets when his sexual tormenter was finally arrested. Dave had been eating out of garbage cans, running afoul of the law, and trying to numb the terrible memories with alcohol and drugs. His life fell apart one day when he was a seven-year-old Cub Scout and his Scout leader began sexually molesting him. Now sixteen, Dave is still on a path of self-destruction, and there is seemingly little his heartbroken mother can do.

Horrific stories of the victims of child sexual abuse serve as lucid reminders that pedophilia is not merely an academic issue to be debated by scholars, but a crime that destroys young lives. Yet allies of the pedophile movement within the scholarly community are attempting to justify men using boys to fulfill their unnatural sexual compulsions.

111

No evidence shows that Alec Walker sought underage boys as sexual partners, and hence this chapter is a diversion from his personal story. The importance of this topic lies in the fact that, despite efforts by homosexual activists to distance the gay lifestyle from pedophilia, there remains a disturbing connection between the two. This is because, by definition, male homosexuals are sexually attracted to other males. While many homosexuals (such as Alec) may not seek young sexual partners, the evidence indicates that disproportionate numbers of gay men seek adolescent males or boys as sexual partners. Note the following evidence that links homosexuality and pedophilia.

Almost All Pedophiles Are Males

An essay on adult sex offenders in the book *Sexual Offending Against Children* reported, "It is widely believed that the vast majority of sexual abuse is perpetrated by males and that female sex offenders only account for a tiny proportion of offences. Indeed, with 3,000 adult male sex offenders in prison in England and Wales at any one time, the corresponding figure for female sex offenders is 12!"[1] This finding was echoed in a report by the American Professional Society on the Abuse of Children, which stated, "In both clinical and non-clinical samples, the vast majority of offenders are male."[2]

Boys Comprise a Significant Percentage of Pedophile Victims

According to the *Journal of Child Psychiatry*, "contemporary studies now indicate that the ratio of girls to boys abused has narrowed remarkably. . . . The majority of community studies suggest a . . . ratio . . . in the order of two to four girls to one boy."[3] Similarly, a study of 457 male sex offenders against children in *Journal of Sex & Marital Therapy* found that "approximately one-third of these sexual offenders directed their sexual activity against males."[4]

Homosexuals Comprise
Less than Three Percent of the Population

Relying upon three large data sets—the General Social Survey, the National Health and Social Life Survey, and the U.S. census—a recent study in *Demography* estimates the number of exclusive male homosexuals in the general population at 2.5 percent and the number of exclusive lesbians at 1.4 percent.[5]

These findings were confirmed by a study of the sexual behavior of men in the United States based on the National Survey of Men (a nationally representative sample comprised of 3,321 men aged twenty to thirty-nine, published in *Family Planning Perspectives*). The study found that "2 percent of sexually active men aged twenty to thirty-nine . . . had had any same-gender sexual activity during the last ten years. Approximately 1 percent of the men (1.3 percent among whites and 0.2 percent among blacks) reported having had exclusively homosexual activity."[6]

Homosexual Pedophiles Are
Overrepresented in Child Sex Abuse Cases

Homosexual pedophiles sexually molest children at a far greater rate than homosexuals in the general population. The above noted study in the *Journal of Sex Research,* which found that one-third of child sex offenders had victimized boys, also reported,"Interestingly, this ratio differs substantially from the ratio of gynephiles (men who erotically prefer physically mature females) to androphiles (men who erotically prefer physically mature males), which is at least 20 to 1."[7]

In other words, although heterosexuals outnumber homosexuals by a ratio of at least 20 to 1, homosexual pedophiles commit about one-third of the total number of child sex offenses.

The *Archives of Sexual Behavior* also noted that homosexual pedophiles are significantly overrepresented in child sex offense cases: "The best epidemiological evidence indicates that only 2 to 4 percent of men attracted to adults prefer men; . . . in contrast, around 25 to 40 percent of men attracted to children prefer boys. *Thus, the rate of homosexual attraction is six to twenty times higher among pedophiles.*"[8]

Are Men Who Molest Boys Really Homosexuals?

Homosexual apologists insist on a simplistic stereotype of pedophilia, which insists that men who molest boys cannot be considered homosexual if they have at any time been married or sexually involved with women. However, the terms *homosexual* and *pedophile* are not mutually exclusive: they describe two intersecting types of sexual attraction.

Webster's Dictionary defines *homosexual* as someone who is sexually attracted to persons of the same sex. *Pedophile* is defined as "an adult who is sexually attracted to young children." The former definition refers to the *gender* of the desired sexual object, while the latter refers to the *age* of the desired sexual object. A male "homosexual pedophile," then, is defined as someone who is generally (but not exclusively, see below) sexually attracted to boys, while a female "homosexual pedophile" is sexually attracted to girls.

The term *homosexual pedophile* was first used in the early twentieth century by the Viennese psychiatrist Richard von Krafft-Ebing, who pioneered the systematic study of sexual deviance. Krafft-Ebing described pedophiles as heterosexually, homosexually, or bisexually oriented. This division has been accepted by pedophiles themselves,[9] and is well attested in the literature.[10]

The Wide-Ranging Sexual Behavior of Homosexuals and Homosexual Pedophiles

The rigid, narrow definition of the terms *homosexual* and *pedophile* that permits no overlap of the terms defies the complex nature of pedophilia. Researchers have long been aware that pedophiles exhibit a wide variety of sexual attractions and behavior—often to draw attention away from their primary lust for boys. A study on sex offenders in the *International Journal of Offender Therapy and Comparative Criminology* notes that "the reason child sexual abusers are successful at remaining undetected is because they do not fit a stereotype."[11]

The data indicates that both homosexuality and pedophilia are intersecting categories that admit to a wide variety of sexual behavior. A study in *Archives of Sexual Behavior* found that homosexual men are attracted to young males. The study compared the sexual age preferences of heterosexual men, heterosexual women, homosexual men, and lesbians. The results showed that, in marked contrast to the other three categories, "all but nine of the forty-eight homosexual men preferred the youngest two male age categories," which included males as young as age fifteen.[12]

In *The Gay Report,* homosexual researchers Karla Jay and Allen Young report data showing that 73 percent of homosexuals surveyed had at some time had sex with boys sixteen to nineteen years of age or younger.[13]

Conversely, homosexual pedophiles are often attracted to adult males. A study of sex offenders against male children in *Behavior Research and Therapy* found that male homosexual pedophiles are sexually attracted to "males of all ages." Compared to nonoffenders, the offenders showed "greater arousal" to slides of nude males as old as twenty-four: "As a group, the child molesters responded [*sic*] with moderate sexual arousal . . . to the nude males of all ages."[14] Similarly, a study of Canadians imprisoned for pedophilia in the *Journal of Interpersonal Violence* noted that some of the adult male offenders also engaged in homosexual acts with adult males.[15]

Many pedophiles, in fact, consider themselves to be homosexual. A study of 229 convicted child molesters in *Archives of Sexual Behavior* found that "86 percent of offenders against males described themselves as homosexual or bisexual."[16]

Further refutation of the narrow definition of the term *pedophile* insisted upon by homosexual activists is the fact that many pedophiles, while primarily sexually attracted to children, also have sexual relationships with women, marry, and father children. A study in *Child Abuse and Neglect* found that 48 percent of the offenders either were married or had been married at some time.[17]

The *Journal of Interpersonal Violence* studied the sexual preferences of male pedophiles who sexually abused children. When they compared the sexual response of the pedophiles with the control group, they found, unexpectedly,"Surprisingly, the two groups did not differ in their response to the nude female stimuli."[18] Another study in the *Psychiatric Journal of the University of Ottawa* reported that "most of the middle-aged pedophiles have had significant adult sexual activity."[19]

Thus, the evidence shows that homosexual pedophiles cannot be narrowly defined as individuals who are solely attracted to underage boys. In fact there is considerable overlap between homosexuality and pedophilia.

Pedophilia in Gay Culture

David Thorstad, homosexual activist and historian of the gay rights movement, argues that there is a natural and undeniable connection between homosexuality and pedophilia. He expresses bitterness that the gay rights movement has, in his view, abandoned pedophilia. Thorstad writes, "Boy-lovers were involved in the gay movement from the beginning, and their presence was tolerated. Gay youth groups encouraged adults to attend their dances. . . . There was a mood of tolerance, even joy at discovering the myriad of lifestyles within the gay and lesbian subculture."[20]

The inaugural issue of the *Gay Community News* in 1979 published a "Statement to the Gay Liberation Movement on the Issue of Man/Boy Love," which challenged the movement to return to a vision of sexual liberation. It argued that "the ultimate goal of gay liberation is the achievement of sexual freedom for all—not just equal rights for 'lesbian and gay men,' but also freedom of sexual expression for young people and children."

Thorstad claims that by 1985 homosexual pedophiles had won acceptance within the gay movement. He cites Jim Kepner, then curator of the International Gay and Lesbian Archives in Los Angeles: "A point I've been trying to make is that if we reject the boy-lovers in our midst today we'd better stop waving the banner of the Ancient Greeks, of Michelangelo, Leonardo da Vinci, Oscar Wilde, Walt Whitman, Horatio Alger, and Shakespeare. We'd better stop claiming them as part of our heritage unless we are broadening our concept of what it means to be gay today."[21]

In 1985 The North American Man/Boy Love Association (NAMBLA) was admitted as a member in New York's council of Lesbian and Gay Organizations as well as the International Gay Association—now the International Lesbian and Gay Association (ILGA). In the mid-1990s, ILGA's association with NAMBLA and other pedophile groups cost the organization its status as a nongovernmental organization in the United Nations.

ILGA's renewed attempt to gain admittance to the UN was rejected again in April 2002 because the organization "did not document that it had purged pedophile groups such as [NAM-BLA]." The *Washington Times* reports that Ishtiag H. Anrabi, Pakistani delegate to the UN Economic and Social Council, expressed concern that ILGA was continuing to be secretive about ties with pedophile groups: "For more than a year, the ILGA has refused to provide documentation or allow review of its membership list to demonstrate that pedophilia groups have been expelled."[22]

Pedophile Themes Abound in Gay Literature

The late "beat" poet and noted homosexual Allen Ginsberg illustrates the seamless connection between homosexuality and pedophilia. Biographer Raymond-Jean Frontain laments the fact that Ginsberg's biographers failed to discuss his poems that contained pederastic themes: "Although both Shumacher and Barry Miles (Ginsberg's initial biographer) frankly discuss Ginsberg's sexual politics, neither refers to his involvement with the controversial North American Man/Boy Love Association. . . . I reread Collected Poems and Ginsberg's two subsequent collections, surprised by the pattern of references to anal intercourse and to pederasty that emerged."[23]

Ginsberg was one of the first of a growing number of homosexual writers who cater to the fascination with pedophilia in the gay community. Mary Eberstadt, writing in the *Weekly Standard,* documents how the taboo against sex with children continues to erode—with the impetus coming from homosexual writers.[24]

Revealingly, the examples she provides of pedophilia in current literature come from gay fiction. Eberstadt cites the *Village Voice,* which states that "gay fiction is rich with idyllic accounts of 'intergenerational relationships,' as such affairs are respectfully called these days."[25] She lists numerous examples of pedophilia-themed gay fiction that appear in "mainstream" homosexual anthologies. *The Gay Canon: Great Books Every Gay Man Should Read* features novels containing scenes of man-boy sex.

One such book is praised as "an operatic adventure into the realms of love, personality, ambition and art . . . a pure joy to read." The protagonist is "a pedophile's dream: the mind of a man in the body of a boy."[26] Another novel which includes graphic descriptions of sexual violence against boys is said to "[tear] straight to the heart of one of the greatest sources, community-wide, of 1990s gay angst: What to do with men who love boys?"[27]

Yet another anthology of homosexual fiction, *A History of Gay Literature: The Male Tradition,* published by Yale University Press, includes "a longish chapter on 'Boys and Boyhood' which is a seemingly definitive account of pro-pedophile literary works."[28] The author appears more concerned with the feelings and emotions of the man than with his boy victim. He explores the question of "whether or not you regard [having sex with boys] as a way of retreating from life or, on the contrary, *as a way of engaging with it at its most honest and least corrupted level.*"[29]

A significant percentage of books that have appeared on the Gay Men's Press fiction bestseller list contain pedophilia themes. Titles include *Some Boys,* described as a "memoir of a lover of boys" that "evokes the author's young friends across four decades;"[30] *For a Lost Soldier,* which tells the story of a sexual relationship between a soldier and an eleven-year-old boy;[31] and *A Good Start, Considering*—yet another story about an eleven-year-old boy (!) who suffers sexual abuse but is rescued by a teenager who "offers him love and affection."[32]

A number of nonfiction publications lend a scholarly veneer to the fascination with pedophilia in the gay community. Such publications attempt to make the case for "intergenerational intimacy." The nation's largest gay publisher, Alyson Publications, which distributes *Daddy's Roommate* and other homosexual books that promote homosexuality to children, publishes books advocating man-boy sex.

One such book, *Paedophilia: The Radical Case,* contains detailed information on how to engage in sexual relations with young boys.[33] Another, *The Age Taboo,* claims, "Boy-lovers . . . are not child molesters. The child abusers are . . . parents who force their staid morality onto the young people in their custody."[34]

Some homosexual commentators have candidly admitted that an inordinate fascination with pedophilia exists within the gay community. Lesbian columnist Paula Martinac, writing in the homosexual newspaper *Washington Blade,* states, "Some gay men still maintain that an adult who has same-sex relations with someone under the legal age of consent is on some level doing the kid a favor by helping to bring him or her 'out.' It's not pedophilia, this thinking goes—pedophilia refers only to *little* kids. Instead, adult-youth sex is viewed as an important aspect of gay culture, with a history dating back to 'Greek love' of ancient times. This romanticized version of adult-youth sexual relations has been a staple of gay literature and has made appearances, too, in gay-themed films."[35]

Martinac adds that "when some gay men venerate adult-youth sex as affirming while simultaneously declaring 'We're not pedophiles,' they send an inconsistent message to society. . . . The lesbian and gay community will never be successful in fighting the pedophile stereotype until we all stop condoning sex with young people."[36]

The Tragic Consequences of Homosexual Child Abuse

Perhaps the most tragic aspect of the homosexual-pedophile connection is the fact that men who sexually molest boys all too often lead their victims into homosexuality and pedophilia. The evidence indicates that a high percentage of homosexuals and pedophiles were themselves sexually abused as children. The *Archives of Sexual Behavior* reports, "One of the most salient findings of this study is that 46 percent of homosexual men and 22 percent of homosexual women reported having been molested by a person of the same gender. This contrasts to only 7 percent of heterosexual men and 1 percent of heterosexual women reporting having been molested by a person of the same gender."[37]

Another study of 279 homosexual/bisexual men with AIDS in the *Journal of the American Medical Association* reported, "More than half of both case and control patients reported a sexual act with a male by age sixteen years, approximately 20 percent by age ten years."[38]

Noted child sex abuse expert David Finkelhor found that "boys victimized by older men were over four times more likely to be currently engaged in homosexual activity than were non-victims. The finding applied to nearly half the boys who had had such an experience. . . . Further, the adolescents themselves often linked their homosexuality to their sexual victimization experiences."[39]

The circle of abuse is the tragic legacy of the attempts by homosexuals to legitimize having sex with boys. For many boys it is already too late to protect them from those who took advantage of their need for love and attention. All too many later perpetrate the abuse by engaging in the sexual abuse of boys. Only by exposing the lies and insincere denials—including those wrapped in scholastic garb—of those who prey sexually on children can we hope to build a wall of protection around the vulnerable youths among us.

CHAPTER 11

Can Homosexuals Change?

I N GRACIOUSLY AGREEING TO be interviewed for this book, Rachel Walker shared openly about the tragic events leading to her husband's death. I offered to substitute a pseudonym for Alec if having the story of his homosexuality and struggle with AIDS appear in print proved to be too difficult for the family.

Rachel initially responded with characteristic magnanimity: "You do not need to change the names. We are quite comfortable talking about it openly and have found that with the passing of the years, it is not so painful any more." However, upon reviewing the manuscript, Rachel changed her mind and asked that I not use the name of her husband and herself.

What caused Rachel's change of heart? In her reply to me, the heart of her objection was that I "portray homosexuality or bisexuality as immoral and a sin. This is totally wrong in my judgment and I will not allow Alec's or our family's name to be used in this way. . . . I totally disagree with your premise, your biblical findings, and your entire approach."

I was troubled that someone who had been so harmed by the homosexual lifestyle found it difficult to confront the true "guilty party." In my response to Rachel I thanked her for sharing her memories, assuring her that I would change names and places wherever possible. I also expressed my concerns:

> You have been blessed with a rich Christian heritage, with your father having served for so long in the ministry. Thus I hope you will not consider me presumptuous by quoting a Bible verse that you surely already know: "Woe to those who call evil good and good evil, who put darkness for light and light for darkness, who put bitter for sweet and sweet for bitter" (Isa. 5:20).

> Rachel, my question is, What is really "wrong" in all of this? Is it the effort to expose the truth about a sexual behavior that is morally wrong, destructive to families, and ultimately deadly? Or was it in fact morally wrong for Alec to violate his marriage vows to you and be sexually unfaithful to you all those years, causing you and the children great emotional pain and cutting short your life together?

> When you deny that his behavior was morally wrong, are you not saying it was "OK" for him to be unfaithful to you? (If it is not morally wrong, then is it not acceptable—or "OK"?) Are you not also implying it was "OK" for him to attempt to sexually seduce me because he was "born" that way?

> I am sure that Alec would not have knowingly infected anyone with HIV. However, do you have the assurance that none of Alec's sexual partners died of AIDS or any other STD, perhaps acquired during the years that Alec had HIV/AIDS, was still seemingly healthy, and was living in denial?

> Behavior that may have led young men to an early grave cannot be considered morally acceptable. Even if Alec did not know for certain that he had AIDS, willful ignorance is no excuse. He was doubtlessly aware of

the AIDS epidemic, which was widely known by the early 1980s. He must have known the risks to himself and to others—even if he chose to ignore them.

Alec would have also borne some responsibility for young men being confirmed in the gay lifestyle instead of getting married, having children, and enjoying family life as intended by God.

I cannot help but wonder, Rachel, if in your heart of hearts you realize you were desperately wronged by the gay lifestyle. And I must believe that your heart's desire would have been to have had a long, faithful marriage together with Alec, and that even today he would be by your side. These inner longings are true and right. It is the path that God intended, and barring other unforeseen circumstances, in His mercy would have come to pass.

I take no pleasure in stirring up painful wounds from the past. I am very sorry that in the later years of your life you do not have your husband. But what stole him from you?

Should not any anger rightfully be directed against Alec's lovers, who were partners in deceit and marital adultery and even more so against efforts to promote and glorify homosexuality in our culture?

Rachel did not reply to my letter. While I did not expect a response, I do hope that she will consider the inconsistency and illogical ramifications believing that homosexual behavior is "OK."

Born or Bred?

During our correspondence, Rachel expressed her firm conviction that her husband did not choose his homosexuality, but rather it was something he was born with. Thus, she did have one wish regarding the book: "The main thing that I ask of you is to respect our firm belief that Alec was born with a genetic inclination toward bisexuality and that he did not act upon it or even know it was there for about forty years of his life. It is not something that he chose to do, nor is it something that he could change or 'cure.' It was part of his makeup, and he struggled to do the best he could to be a supportive father and husband and friend, and to balance it all in the one big circle of life."

On this sensitive topic Rachel and I must unfortunately agree to disagree. In this chapter I will attempt to show why I do not believe homosexuality is "inborn." However, Rachel and I may be closer than we realize regarding the heart of many people's concern about this issue.

Homosexuals are angered by the attitude that gays and lesbians "choose" to become homosexuals—as if they simply woke up one morning and "decided" to enter the gay lifestyle. Why, they say, would anyone "choose" to embark upon a life fraught with such confusion and pain, not to mention societal rejection and hostility? What about the homosexual inclinations that were evident even in their earliest childhood memories?

In this I can agree and sympathize with those who are enraged that anyone could think that what is so deeply a part of their very being is the result of some frivolous decision to defy moral convention.

I also agree that certain personalities may predispose an individual to be more sensitive to gender confusion. Those born with especially sensitive natures, for example, may react to emotional trauma suffered at an early age in ways that, if unchecked, may make them vulnerable to a wide variety of aberrant behavior, including homosexuality. Such individuals quite understandably feel that they were "born" with abnormal attractions to the same sex. Yet their feelings are not proof that homosexuality is inborn: it simply demonstrates that in many cases homosexual feelings arise at an early age.

It would be difficult to gauge how the divorce of his parents and the effective loss of his father influenced the young Alec's sexual development. According to Rachel, "Alec did not identify with his stepfather. Frank was brusque and rough and blunt and did not treat his mother very well. His birth father was a good man, but not very present in his life. From [the time Alec was] seven on, his father was in the war."

Alec harbored warm memories of his father. Alec Sr. was well liked by everyone: he would laugh and play with his children. His nickname was "Brooksie." In what may have been a way of identifying with his absent father, Alec sometimes went by that name as well. When Alec was seventeen, his father died of a heart attack. It must have been a keenly felt loss for the young Alec, who was living with relatives. One can only imagine the sadness and longing he felt for the father he barely knew.

Who, then, served as a masculine role model for the young Alec? Rachel relates that in the absence of his real father, Alec identified most closely with his mother's brother, Uncle John. Uncle John gave Alec nice secondhand clothes—including his first suit—and took an interest in his progress. But while an uncle can show kindness and help soothe a boy's wounded spirit, in many ways there is no replacement for a father.

We must have compassion for those whose suffering in their early years has caused emotional and sexual confusion. But as for adults who engage in homosexual behavior, there is another vital consideration—that each of us are free moral agents. We've all heard those who claim they "can't keep themselves" from illicit drug use, excessive drinking—even adultery—because they were "born" with what they claim are uncontrollable proclivities. While Scripture teaches that we are born with fallen natures that incline us toward any number of vices, it does not permit us to excuse any particular inclination as inevitable or uncontrollable.

While we all have "tendencies" or weaknesses, each of us has at least some capacity to strive against wrong or harmful urges.

We may have strength enough only to cry out to God for help, but He will hear and honor that request.

To deny that victory over temptation is possible is to deny the scriptural promise: "No temptation has seized you except what is common to man. And God is faithful; he will not let you be tempted beyond what you can bear. But when you are tempted, he will also provide a way out so that you can stand up under it" (1 Cor. 10:13 NIV).

No exceptions are listed in this verse. We are not "programmed" or hopelessly forced to engage in any illicit or dangerous practices. Those struggling with homosexual tendencies or other forms of temptation may avail themselves of the divine assistance promised in Scripture.

Victory is possible. For every young man born into an impoverished, broken home and who becomes involved in illegal drugs, there are others who resist such temptations, choosing the right path. For every person who dies an early death from alcoholism, others gain the victory over the bottle. For every husband who surrenders to the "irresistible" enticement of sexual lust, many others learn to control such temptations and live faithful, monogamous lives.

As we have suggested, the causes of homosexual feelings appear to be manifold, but despite media reports in recent years that often present scientific evidence in selective sound bites, to date there exists no clear proof for a genetic origin of homosexuality. Let's examine the supposed evidence that a "gay gene" exists.

The Hamer Study

A flurry of media reports in 1993 indicated that scientists had at long last discovered a gay gene. The reports were based on the work of geneticist Dean Hamer of the National Cancer Institute. Hamer, however, never claimed to have found a gene that inevitably determines that a person will be homosexual. Rather, he claimed to have located a genetic component to some instances of male homosexuality.[1]

After studying forty pairs of brothers who were homosexual, Hamer hypothesized that a certain genetic marker on the X chromosome was at least partially responsible for their homosexuality. Since men have an X and a Y chromosome, and they inherit their X chromosome from their mothers, Hamer theorized that the mother may be the carrier of the gene determining homosexuality in their sons. Homosexual behavior would not be manifested in the mothers' lives, but they would pass that gene on to their sons.

Of the families Hamer interviewed that had more than one son who was homosexual, a significantly larger number had a maternal uncle or a maternal aunt's son who was also homosexual. By comparison, the links with paternal linkage were weaker. This would suggest a maternal linkage for male homosexuality in some cases. Finding homosexual brothers who had homosexual maternal uncles would indicate that the gene determining homosexuality was transmitted through the mother's family line. Hamer wrote in his report, "We have now produced evidence that one form of male homosexuality is preferentially transmitted through the maternal side and is genetically linked to chromosomal region Xq28."[2]

Hamer's study is known as a "linkage" study, where researchers isolate traits found in an extended family and then look for a common DNA segment, or marker, on a particular chromosome. If the same marker is present consistently in the family members who have that trait, it is theorized that the marker may be the gene that causes—or "codes"—for that trait. Linkage studies have successfully located genes that cause Huntington's disease, cystic fibrosis, and muscular dystrophy. However, to date linkage studies have not found genes that code for complex behaviors.

Upon closer examination, Hamer's study raised more questions than it answered. For example, seven sets of homosexual brothers did not display the genetic variants Hamer theorized led to homosexuality. In attempting to explain this anomaly, Hamer mentioned the possibility of "nongenetic sources of variation in sexual orientation"—in other words, a nongenetic origin of homosexuality.[3]

Questions were raised about Hamer's methodology, such as the absence of a randomly selected control group. The Office of Research Integrity of the Department of Health and Human Services investigated Hamer when one of his research assistants claimed that he withheld findings that were inconsistent with his conclusions. The results of the investigation were never released. However, it is known that the National Cancer Institute transferred Hamer to the National Institutes of Health.

Hamer's Study Was Not Replicated

Before being accepted as accurate, the results of a scientific study must be reproduced by other studies. The Hamer study, however, has not been validated by follow-up studies. Drs. George Rice and George Ebers of the University of Western Ontario attempted unsuccessfully to reproduce Hamer's results. They found that only about 50 percent of homosexual brothers shared the same genetic variants—far less than the high correlation that Hamer allegedly found.

Rice and Ebers's study, which appeared in the April 1999 issue of *Science* magazine, the same magazine that years earlier had published Hamer's study, concluded, "These results do not support an X-linked gene underlying male homosexuality."[4] The authors continued: "It is unclear why our results are so discrepant from Hamer's original study. Because our study was larger than that of Hamer et al., we certainly had adequate power to detect a genetic effect as large as was reported in that study. Nonetheless, our data do not support the presence of a gene of large effect influencing sexual orientation at position Xq28."[5]

Rewind to the March 1993 edition of the *Archives of General*

Psychiatry, in which Drs. William Byne and Bruce Parsons examined past and current claims and concluded that "there is no evidence at present to substantiate a biologic theory. The appeal of current biologic explanations for sexual orientation may derive more from dissatisfaction with the present status of psychosocial explanations than from a substantiating body of experimental data."[6]

However, the waters were muddied once again by another study, this one of lesbian twins, in the same edition of *Archives.* Conducted by J. Michael Bailey and Richard C. Pillard, the study found that about half the lesbians in the sample had a twin who was lesbian.[7] The authors concluded that lesbianism may have a partly genetic origin.

The Bailey-Pillard study, however, was flawed by a lack of random sampling. The lesbian twins were recruited through advertisements in homosexual publications that, presumably, are read primarily by those who identify with the gay rights movement. In addition, the twins in the study were raised in the same household, making it impossible to rule out environmental and familial factors in the formation of their lesbian identity.

The Bailey-Pillard study actually showed a frequency rate for homosexual siblings similar to that of adoptive siblings with no shared genetic inheritance whatever. The study also failed to take into account factors such as the unique psychological dynamics of twins, age of earliest sexual experiences, and whether one or both of the twins were sexually molested. Finally, the fact that nearly half of the homosexual twins' identical siblings were heterosexual argued strongly against the theory that sexual orientation is genetically based. If that were true, 100 percent of the twins should be homosexual.

The Brain Studies

Another highly publicized study that purported to show that homosexuality was inborn was conducted in 1991 by former Salk Institute researcher Simon LeVay. LeVay studied the brains of thirty-five male cadavers, including ten known homosexuals and sixteen supposedly heterosexual men, and found that a certain region of the brain (a cluster of neurons known as INAH-3, the third interstitial hypothalamus) was generally smaller among the homosexual men.[8]

LeVay's study, however, suffered from serious methodological errors. It had an extremely small sample size and failed to identify a control group. Also, LeVay made questionable assumptions regarding the orientation of the "heterosexual" cadavers. He assumed that they were all heterosexual, even though six of the "heterosexual" subjects had died of AIDS.

Other anomalies of LeVay's study included the fact that three of the "heterosexuals" had brain clusters smaller than the mean size for the homosexuals. On the other hand, three of the homosexuals had larger clusters than the mean size for "heterosexuals." LeVay also gave no explanation as to what role the brain clusters play, if any, in sexual orientation. He also ignored one obvious explanation: that the allegedly smaller brain clusters did not cause homosexuality but were the result of sexual activity or of AIDS-related brain damage.

The Evidence Regarding Lesbianism

Ironically, some of the same researchers who argue for a genetic origin of homosexuality deny that lesbianism is inborn. As evidence that lesbianism is learned behavior, Hamer cites a study by Australian behavioral geneticist Nicolas Martin and J. Michael Bailey.[9] Using a national registry of twins in Australia, the authors studied 1,912 women between the ages of seventeen and fifty. They found no difference in the rate of lesbianism in identical or fraternal twins.

Once again, if there were a genetic factor to lesbianism, the incidence of shared lesbianism would be 100 percent in identical twins (who have an identical genetic makeup). Hamer wrote, "The results showed that for women the main influence on sexual orientation was the shared environment—being raised in the same household by the same parent—while genes seemed to count hardly at all."[10]

Hamer also mentions a study conducted with molecular geneticist Angela Pattatucci, which found that the incidence pattern of lesbianism in families was similar to that of male homosexuality.[11] However, Hamer and Pattatucci concluded that lesbianism could not have been genetically caused. Hamer writes that "the pattern we observed could mean only one thing: being a lesbian, or a non-heterosexual woman, was 'culturally transmitted,' not inherited."[12]

Thus we find a fundamental contradiction in the arguments regarding the origin of homosexuality. On the one hand it is admitted that female homosexuality (lesbianism) is the result of environmental influences, while at the same time it is claimed that male homosexuality is genetically caused and "inborn."

The Stein Critique

Surprisingly, some of the strongest criticism of the "gay gene" hypothesis comes from the homosexual community itself. One such researcher is Edward Stein, Ph.D., author of *The Mismeasure of Desire: The Science, Theory, and Ethics of Sexual Orientation*.[13] Stein critically examines the research of both Hamer and LeVay that claims a biological origin to homosexuality, concluding, "There are serious problems with the science itself. . . . My training had taught me that a lot of what was being said was, well, highly unscientific."[14]

In addition to the criticisms noted above, Stein points out that, despite claims to the contrary, none of the researchers studying the supposed biological origins of homosexuality has proven direct causation. Stein refutes Hamer's claim to have found "one form of homosexuality" transmitted through the maternal line: "Genes in themselves cannot directly specify any behavior or psychological phenomenon. Instead, genes direct a particular pattern of RNA synthesis, which in turn may influence the development of psychological dispositions and the expression of behaviors.

There are necessarily many intervening pathways between a gene and a disposition or a behavior, and even more intervening variables between a gene and a pattern that involves both thinking and behaving. The terms 'gay gene' and 'homosexual gene' are, therefore, without meaning. . . . No one has . . . presented evidence in support of such a simple and direct link between genes and sexual orientation."[15]

As for Simon LeVay, Stein rejects his claim that "children may already be determined to become homosexual or heterosexual."[16] Stein writes, "LeVay has at best shown that there is a *correlation* between INAH-3 and sexual orientation; he has not, as he admits when he is careful, shown any causation. Further, . . . he has no evidence that biological factors directly affect sexual orientation. Even if he could prove that INAH-3 size and sexual orientation are perfectly correlated in his sample population (and I have argued that he fails to do so), this would not establish any direct causal account of homosexuality."[17]

Stein frankly admits efforts to locate a "gay gene" serve to advance the gay political agenda: "Many gay people want to use this research to promote gay rights. If gay people are 'born that way,' then discrimination against them must be wrong. . . . A gay or lesbian person's public identity, sexual behaviors, romantic relationships, or decisions to raise children are all choices. No theory suggests that these choices are genetic."[18]

Once again, this rejection of the theory that homosexuals are "born that way" comes not from a "homophobic antigay fundamentalist," but from a researcher with close ties to the gay community. In his book *My Genes Made Me Do It!*, biochemist Neil Whitehead notes, "Science has not yet discovered any genetically dictated behavior in humans. So far, genetically dictated behaviors of the one-gene-one-trait variety have been found only in very simple organisms."[19]

Similarly, *Science* magazine discussed the failure of efforts to find genetic causes for human behavior: "Time and time again, scientists have claimed that particular genes or chromosomal regions are associated with behavioral traits, only to withdraw their findings when they were not replicated. 'Unfortunately,' says Yale's [Dr. Joel] Gelernter, 'it's hard to come up with many' findings linking specific genes to complex human behaviors that have been replicated. 'All were announced with great fanfare; all were greeted unskeptically in the popular press; all are now in disrepute.'"[20]

Evidence that Homosexuals Can Change

In the absence of reliable evidence for a "gay gene," the obvious cause of homosexual behavior is environmental influences in the life of the individual. And if homosexuality is "learned" behavior, can what is "learned" become "unlearned"?

Until recently the major professional organizations have steadfastly denied that homosexuals can change—a strangely intractable position in an age of emphasis upon human potential and the championing of the right of individuals to choose their behavior.

Yet cracks are beginning to appear. Perhaps influenced by reports of thousands of former homosexuals who have successfully changed their behavior, some have dared to question the dogma that homosexuals can never change. One such voice of momentous significance is Dr. Robert Spitzer, psychiatrist and professor at Columbia University. Back in 1973, Spitzer was a leading force in the American Psychiatric Association's landmark decision to remove homosexuality from its list of pathological behaviors, a decision that had a great role in reshaping society's view of homosexuality.

However, in the years following the APA decision Spitzer became increasingly intrigued by reports that through counseling—termed "reparative therapy"—homosexuals were able to change their behavior. Finally he decided to initiate a study of former homosexuals. He interviewed 153 men and 47 women who reported that they had successfully undergone counseling regarding their unwanted same-sex attraction and had maintained a change in their sexual behavior and fantasies for at least five years.

Spitzer found that, after counseling, 76 percent of the men and 47 percent of women eventually married. Of those, Spitzer found that 66 percent of the men and 44 percent of the women had achieved "good heterosexual functioning." The vast majority of the participants—89 percent of men and 95 percent of women—said they were bothered only slightly or not at all by unwanted homosexual feelings.

Summarizing his paper, Spitzer wrote, "The subjects' self-reports of change appear to be, by and large, valid, rather than gross exaggerations, brainwashing or wishful thinking. We therefore conclude that some individuals who participate in a sexual-reorientation therapy apparently make sustained changes in sexual orientation."[21]

The reaction from homosexual activists was fast and furious. David Elliot, spokesman for the National Gay and Lesbian Task Force in Washington, claimed, "The sample is terrible, totally tainted, and totally unrepresentative of the gay and lesbian community." Wayne Besen of the homosexual advocacy organization Human Rights Campaign attempted to paint Spitzer as "biased" in his views regarding homosexuality.

Spitzer flatly rejected these allegations, pointing out that as late as 1995 he appeared on the *Geraldo* television show arguing that "sexual orientation" is unchangeable. It was not until he met and spoke with ex-homosexuals, he said, that he decided to conduct a scientific study on the possibility of homosexuals changing their same-sex desires.

Dr. Joseph Nicolosi, a California psychiatrist and the director of the National Association for Research and Therapy of Homosexuality, called Spitzer's study "revolutionary." "The assumption that people can't change is a political conclusion rather than a scientific conclusion," said Nicolosi. "It points to the influential gay lobbyists within the profession, of which there are many. When we issued a study last year saying more than 800 people had changed, it was pushed to the side. But when Spitzer issues this, it has to be listened to because of his track record as a gay advocate."

Appearing on the ABC news program *20/20,* Spitzer rejected suggestions that reparative therapy was a vain attempt to change the unchangeable. Reporter Deborah Roberts asked, "But it sounds like they are suppressing their sexual orientation rather than actually changing it"—to which Spitzer responded, "That's not the way they experienced it. I am personally convinced that for many of them, they made rather remarkable changes in their sexual orientation." Also interviewed was John Westcott, a former homosexual who is now married. Westcott responded to those who would deny the possibility of change: "Some people hate us because if we're living the truth, then they're living a lie."

Logicians know that it takes but a single exception to prove an absolute negative. This is the fatal flaw of radical homosexual activists and their supporters, who dogmatically refuse to admit that anyone can change from being homosexual to heterosexual. But evidence of such change is abundant and increasing.

Implications for the Walkers's Marriage
In addition to the evidence that homosexuality is learned behavior that can be changed and the biblical condemnation of homosexual behavior, the belief that homosexuals are "born that

way" poses difficult ethical and theological questions. Was it God's will that Alec marry Rachel, have children, and also engage in homosexual behavior that ultimately cut short his life and marriage? If Alec was indeed "born gay," then one could properly conclude that "God made him that way." But if God made Alec to find sexual fulfillment in men, then how could it be part of the divine plan for Alec for him to be married to a woman?

To say that Alec was born a homosexual is tantamount to saying that all the love, romance, and commitment that he and Rachel experienced when they fell in love, married, embarked upon a life of service, and started a family was an unfortunate mistake. The union of Alec and Rachel was misguided because Alec was truly meant to find fulfillment with men.

One wholly unsatisfactory way out of this theological and logical dilemma is to claim that Alec was "born" to be "bisexual"—to have sexual relations with both men and women. While this explanation might satisfy the unchurched and irreligious, it can hardly be acceptable to those who believe in a moral order and ethical principles such as marital commitment and faithfulness. The reason is that it assumes marital infidelity is acceptable because "that's how God made him."

Few whose lives are informed by Judeo-Christian ethical principles would accept this reasoning. Even non-Christian cultures have an intuitive understanding that the sexual act is intended for the confines of marriage. Few societies tolerate adultery, yet bisexuality is by definition immoral and (when the individual is married) adulterous behavior, since it involves having sexual relations with more than one person.

The unavoidable conclusion is that Alec Walker was created by God to find sexual and relational fulfillment in a woman, that he and Rachel met and married by "divine appointment," and that the potential existed for a long and happy life together. Yet something conspired to thwart that plan—something went desperately wrong. The origins of that dark obsession may be unknown, but the result was that at some point Alec entered into the homosexual lifestyle with ultimately tragic results.

One passage in the Walkers's account of their Peace Corps service in Ecuador has stuck in my mind. Rachel tells about the preparations for Alec's thirtieth birthday party, which turned into a major social event in the poor seaside neighborhood where they lived. Literally hundreds of people showed up for the festivities, which involved eating, drinking, and dancing through the night. Alec was delayed.

> "Where is Alec?" they shouted, and a surge of voices calling Alec's name became a deafening roar. "Alec, Alec!" . . . Suddenly I felt a strong arm around my waist and there he was at my side, giving me a mighty squeeze. Alec's handsome, sun-tanned face was ablaze with excitement as he waved to the crown of cheering neighbors. "Viva Santo!" they shouted over and over again. "Long live the birthday saint!" A wave of emotion choked my throat—love for my husband, pride in his rapport with the people, and tremendous affection for our wonderful friends and neighbors of Manta.

The deep love and admiration of Rachel for Alec shines through the words on the page. She doubtlessly had every expectation that their life together would continue. During those days of glorious optimism it would have been inconceivable to think that their marital union would be shaken to the core by sexual infidelity, and that in the prime of their lives this marvelous love story would be cut short by a dark obsession.

CHAPTER 12

The Rest of the Story

THE YEARS PASSED. After graduating from Moody Bible Institute I continued my education, eventually earning my Ph.D. in religion from Marquette University in my hometown of Milwaukee, Wisconsin. Alec and I spoke a few times on the phone, but things had changed. After that evening in the restaurant, when it became clear to him that I had no intention of entering into a homosexual relationship, he no longer pursued me.

After completing my education I went to Israel to serve with a Christian ministry. While living and working in Bethlehem, I met my future wife, Rebekka, who had come from Switzerland to volunteer at Bethlehem Bible School, where I was teaching. We were married in Rebekka's home town in Switzerland and returned to Israel to spend several more years, during which time we had two children. Another son followed when we left Israel and lived for a year in Switzerland. We then came to the states, where our last two children were born. I taught at a Bible college in Georgia before moving to the Washington, D.C., area, where I continued writing and eventually joined the Family Research Council.

During all this time Alec never left my mind. Even though we had lost all contact, I would wonder about him. I attributed my continued interest to the fact that Alec was such a fascinating person. I was curious about what had happened in his life all these years. But in reality I suppose I was hoping to recapture just one more glimpse of the fatherly attention he showered on me.

At long last my curiosity got the better of me. I began searching for what I could learn about Alec. I purchased a rare used copy of the Walkers's biography of their life in Ecuador. An Internet database search brought up an interview with the Walkers conducted years after I last saw them. I learned that Alec had given up his prestigious executive position and returned with his family to South America in service with the Peace Corps—this time as codirector for Chile and Belize. Alec held the diplomatic rank of Counselor-Senior Foreign Service in Brazil. I saw the distinctive mark of Alec in this new knowledge: how characteristic of him to leave his comfortable, lucrative position and strike out in some exciting venture. I tried to imagine an Alec of the present. Was his vigor and enthusiasm for life still undiminished?

I decided to try to contact Alec and was assisted by the marvels of technology. An Internet search showed a telephone listing for a "Walker" in the Minneapolis area. Now all that remained was picking up the phone. I hesitated for days, telling myself it was a foolish idea. Let bygones be bygones. Alec wouldn't remember me and I'd just be embarrassed. Or worse—would he coldly reject me?

But I'd come this far and knew I had to follow through. Finally, I picked up the phone and dialed. Someone answered.

"Hello?" A young woman with a slight accent was on the other end. Could it be Juanita? The last I saw the Walkers's adopted daughter from Ecuador, she was a bouncy little girl. I had no idea how to proceed.

"Is this the Walker residence?" I asked.

"Yes, it is."

I decided to jump in. I explained that I was an old friend of Alec's, asking, "Is this by any chance Juanita?" She said it was.

"I was wondering . . .," I fumbled. "Is Alec . . . ?" *How do you ask if someone is still alive?*

"Alec died," Juanita said simply.

The words, so simple, crashed like thunder through my head. Alec, so full of life and vigor, was no more. An inexpressible sadness settled on me. A thousand questions raced through my mind.

"When? Do you mind me asking?"

"Alec died in 1989," said Juanita. I made a mental calculation. Alec must have died in his late 50s. What snuffed out his life in the prime of his years? Was it an automobile crash or some other terrible accident, perhaps cancer? But one possible cause of his death seemed more probable than all others. I had to ask and hoped I wasn't being too intrusive.

"Did he—did he die of . . ." I couldn't bring myself to say the words.

"He died of AIDS," volunteered Juanita. I wondered how many other times the Walker family had to endure the same painfully awkward exchange?

An entire canopy of emotions unfolded inside my head. I visualized a progression from vibrant health to a gaunt, wasted form. I didn't press for more details. In the midst of my musings I wondered about Juanita's relationship with her father. I hoped Alec showered his attention on her like he did so many others.

Juanita invited me to call later when Rachel would be home. Rachel! Would she be open to talking about it?

Rachel's Story

That evening she answered when I called back. I caught her at the end of a long day. It was the Rachel I remembered—always busy in numerous civic and cultural affairs. She spoke with me, tired and lying on her bed—their bed.

"Alec died right here in this room, on this bed," Rachel told me matter-of-factly. As I listened I had a flashback of Alec lying on that bed in better days, when he was at the height of his attractiveness.

As we talked, Rachel described how she had first sensed something was wrong in her relationship with Alec. The first warning sign came about fifteen years into their marriage, when Alec invited a young student from Ecuador to live at their home. This was not unusual for Alec and Rachel, who opened their home many times over the years to those in need.

Rachel described the young man from Ecuador as a "great kid" who went to high school in Excelsior and helped around the house. Still, as she put it, she somehow "sensed that Alec and he had a 'special' kind of relationship, although there was never any obvious proof."

Rachel described her red flag: "It was just more of an inkling, and I dismissed it after the young man went back to Ecuador." The fact that the young man had a girlfriend whom he eventually married somewhat eased Rachel's suspicions, and she decided against confronting Alec about it.

But the warning signs continued to pop up. Rachel remembered another young man named John whom Alec befriended. John was "a very good-looking fellow" who had a wife and child. Rachel said John became an obsession for Alec: "We all enjoyed him and his family. However, it was the kind of friendship that consumed Alec. He spent a great deal of time with John, helping him find a job and lots of other things, like an apartment and a car, etc. I don't know if he gave him financial help, but I think he did."

Rachel recalled how, when she tried to share her concerns with Alec about the relationship, he claimed he was only trying to help John find himself. "I liked John well enough," Rachel said graciously, "but I thought that he was too dependent on Alec and drained too much attention away from us and the family. I mentioned this to Alec and he said that he was only try-ing to help a 'diamond in the rough' improve his life."

Rachel decided not to press the issue. After all, it was hard to criticize Alec for helping someone in need: "So again I let it go. But it seemed too intimate and involving for Alec to handle and I was uncomfortable with it. . . . I just didn't like the whole rela-tionship. Alec denied that there was anything out of the ordinary about it at all."

As the years passed Alec continued to be involved in similar kinds of relationships where he helped young men in need. But when he left his high profile executive job in Minneapolis and started his own public relations firm in Washington, D.C., Alec started openly associating with homosexuals. He rented an apart-ment in town while Rachel remained in Minnesota. Washington, D.C., has a large homosexual community, and Rachel soon learned that Alec had male bisexual friends. Rachel remembered Alec's line of reasoning: "He told me over and over, and I agreed with him, that having deep friendships outside of the marriage made the marriage richer and more meaningful for us as a cou-ple." After all, she thought, I have good friendships with women, how can I prevent him from having friendships with men? But Rachel's friendships were platonic, and her feminine intuition warned her that Alec's "friendships" were not.

When Alec decided to serve another term in South America with the Peace Corps, his extracurricular interests and activities continued. Rachel remembered one "male friend" of Alec's among the Peace Corps volunteers that involved "nothing overt, but it just felt uncomfortable to me."

By this time Alec could no longer deny his involvement with homosexuals. When Rachel asked him about his male friends, he admitted that they were gay—but he never admitted he had a sexual relationship with any of them. "It was an unspoken topic," said Rachel. "I felt uncomfortable about it, but I couldn't fight it. I accepted it as I loved Alec deeply, and we had a good family life and a fine togetherness as a couple. I wanted to stay with him and never once entertained the idea of a separation or divorce. The positive outweighed the negative. It was all part of the whole picture. We had been married for thirty-one years when he died."

While genuinely admiring her dedication to Alec and to their marriage, I wondered about her statement that "the positive outweighed the negative." In many ways Alec and Rachel had a wonderful, exciting life together, but sexual unfaithfulness is uniquely destructive to a marriage relationship. Marriages that endure financial, health, and numerous other kinds of problems often flounder when one or both of the spouses commit adultery. The reason is that the sexual union is the most intimate of human relationships, described in Scripture as "becoming one flesh." The act of adultery violates that sacred bond and thus strikes at the heart of that sacred relationship.

I wonder what Rachel's response would have been if Alec had committed adultery with another woman? I believe that she, like most wives, would have demanded that the infidelity stop—or else. She would not have excused the sexual betrayal on the rationale that "overall, the marriage is good."

That being said, some women are faced with a very difficult choice: either put up with a husband that has no intention of changing his adulterous ways or suffer the breakup of a family. That many such women choose to remain in the marriage for the sake of the children and hope the husband will reform may be viewed as selfless dedication to their marriage, but it does not excuse the incorrigible behavior of their husbands.

Alec's Battle with AIDS

In 1983, after returning from their second stint with the Peace Corps, Rachel began to be concerned about Alec's health. He wasn't feeling well and apparently had no idea what was wrong. He was losing weight and began having problems with his digestive system. Visits to doctors brought little relief. This was in the early stages of the AIDS epidemic, when the medical community had not yet come to grips with the magnitude of the looming crisis. Since no outward signs of the disease were manifest, Alec chose not to have any blood tests done.

Then one day Rachel read a magazine article about what in those days was called "AIDS Related Complex" or "ARC." The nausea, night sweats, and loss of weight associated with ARC seemed to fit Alec's symptoms. Rachel again asked him to have his condition medically evaluated, but he continued to avoid doctors. His condition was not diagnosed until 1987, when he was admitted into the hospital for pneumonia. While there, blood tests removed all doubt that Alec had full-blown AIDS.

The doctors told Alec that he had been living with HIV for as long as ten years. Rachel suspects that he may have been infected as early as 1979 while living a "bachelor life" among the gay community of Washington, D.C. At that time the first cases of HIV—which were thought to have originated from Africa—appeared on the East Coast.

Rachel then had to face the possibility that she may have contracted HIV, since she and Alec continued to have sexual relations during the years that Alec was infected but not diagnosed. She had a blood test and was greatly relieved when it came back negative. Her concern continued, and it wasn't until several more tests were conducted that she could rest assured that she had not contracted HIV.

I asked Rachel about her emotions upon learning that Alec had AIDS. She replied poignantly, "My response was one of great sadness. I didn't want him to die. I wanted our marriage to go on and for us to have a long old age together." Since Alec could not bring himself to admit he had AIDS, it fell upon Rachel to inform their children: "I told each of our children individually in their own homes at their own kitchen tables." By this time three of the Walkers's children were married, and their youngest daughter was still in college. Their responses to the devastating news ranged from disbelief to sadness to anger.

Alec remained in denial until the end. Rachel reported that he refused to discuss his illness and never once admitted, "I have AIDS." Instead, he would tell others that he had pneumonia or pancreatitis (a chronic and painful infection of the pancreas common to AIDS patients) or some other ailment that was related to AIDS. During Alec's last months Rachel and their children attended support groups for families of AIDS patients. Alec took an interest in what was discussed at these sessions. Rachel said, "We found that most of the people in the group were experiencing the same situations . . . the AIDS person never really talking openly about it but finding great solace in the care and concern of others."

Alec gave little indication that he knew he was dying, remaining hopeful to the end. Even though he participated in discussions with Rachel about funeral arrangements, such as cremation and details about the service and music, he still thought he would get better. Speaking of the pancreatitis that afflicted him, he voiced confidence that he would yet "lick this thing."

As Alec's condition deteriorated, it was left to Rachel to call Alec's extended family and tell them he was dying, explaining that if they wanted to see him, they had better come soon.

Carlos, who was then serving in the Marine Corps, obtained a leave of absence and moved back home from California to take care of his father. Their family stayed for the final seven weeks of Alec's life, making it possible for Rachel to continue her teaching job. All of Alec's children came home to be with him in his final days.

As he began to fade in and out of consciousness, Alec had private talks with Drew and Carlos. He did not have any dying words, although, as Rachel remembers his last hours: "We knew and he knew that we loved him and he loved us. We all told him verbally that we loved him in his final hours, and his sweet response was a filling of his eyes and tears overflowing down his cheeks."

Rachel believes that, as with so many people suffering from AIDS, Alec was ashamed and embarrassed about how thin and gaunt he had become: "Alec was always rather vain about his appearance." Still, the charismatic Alec that I remembered was evident up to the last: "He had a great personality, good wit and [was] full of humor and kindness," said Rachel. "This never changed. He was gracious to all who came to see him." In his last days, his cousins from Kentucky came to see him. Alec announced that he wanted a "tea party" in his bedroom. But by the time everything was prepared, he had fallen asleep.

As he approached death's door, Alec gave little indication of what he thought awaited him on the other side. But in an unguarded moment he remarked to Rachel about "going way out there." Hearing that reminded me of a similar remark by actor Michael Landon as he lay dying of pancreatic cancer: the stricken actor said he was anxious to be released from his body of pain and to "fly away."

While it may be pleasant to imagine death as a release from all earthly restraint to soar at will into the heavens, the Bible tells us what follows this life: "Just as man is destined to die once, and after that to face judgment" (Heb. 9:27 NIV). Humans are not autonomous beings, "free" to roam the skies at will after this life; rather, each of us will answer to God: "For we will all stand before God's judgment seat. It is written: 'As surely as I live,' says the Lord, 'every knee will bow before me; every tongue will confess to God.' So then, each of us will give an account of himself to God" (Rom. 14:10b–12 NIV).

Alec George Walker died on Monday, April 17, 1989. He was the 300th person in Minnesota to die of AIDS.

Rachel expressed regret that Alec was unable to discuss his condition and share with his family on a deeper level: "If he had been more open to talking about AIDS to people, he would have had a better chance to discuss the issues and change his philosophy. But he never did. Maybe in his own heart, but not overtly. He did talk with our minister and that was good. He talked with me, but always in a covert way, not openly."

Rachel summarized her husband: "He was a loving and gracious person who was popular with all in his life, but carried many secrets in his heart that he never shared. If he had been able to be more open with his loved ones, especially his children, he and they would have had a more meaningful relationship in the end. But it never happened. They knew he loved them, and he knew they loved him. That was not the problem. He just was not open and revealing to them and they could not get through his facade. The deep sharing never happened. The huge stigma of AIDS was impossible for him to break through."

One final casualty of Alec's passing was Marie. She had struggled for years with mood swings and was intermittently on medication. On one occasion Marie had attempted suicide.

Rachel related the reaction of their youngest daughter: "When Alec died, Marie came home and mourned along with us, but she still showed signs of anger and resentment at him for 'doing this to us.'"

After her father's death, Marie couldn't seem to rise above her emotional difficulties. Rachel wrote that Marie "was very sweet to me when I was grieving the loss of Alec and was a dear daughter. She . . . came home to live with me so I wouldn't be alone after Alec died. Marie liked her job, but kept pointing out that she wished she could get a better job, wear nicer clothes and drive a better car. I encouraged her to take it a day at a time and she would find happiness in the fulfillment of the little things of each day. She really felt happiness would never come. Her goal was to 'be a success' by the time she was twenty-five. Marie took her own life three days short of her twenty-fifth birthday." Her beloved father was not there in her hour of greatest need.

Postscript

THIS BOOK IS NOT intended to be an instrument to "bash gays." It is a dirge—a poem of mourning for a gifted, kind, and supremely appealing soul. All these years later the memory of Alec still brings a twinge of pain, which is but a drop in the ocean compared to that suffered by his family and countless other families that have lost loved ones to this dangerous and deadly lifestyle.

The reader may wonder how my experience with Alec affected me. First, I am eternally thankful for how Alec *failed* to influence me. If Alec had succeeded in initiating me into homosexuality, my life would almost certainly have followed the deadly trajectory of innumerable other young men who enter the gay lifestyle. If statistics are any guide, that would have meant a life of promiscuity and disease, followed very likely by premature death.

If Alec had succeeded, I would have become one more face in the gay community, wounded after the inevitable abandonment, yearning for "true love" but never seeming to find it. I have no doubt that my gay relationships would have gradually been of shorter and shorter duration, until I had either settled on a life of quiet desperation and loneliness or abandoned myself to the fleeting pleasures of homosexual promiscuity. And through it all my soul would have been tormented by a guilty conscience and terrified of divine judgment.

I would almost certainly not have had the blessed privilege of meeting and falling in love with my wife, Rebekka, or known the joys of being a father to our five wonderful children. The trials and struggles of life have at times been severe, and I stand in perpetual need of divine grace, but I am wholly content in and devoted to my God-given role as husband and father.

I reject the superficial rejoinder by gay activists that someone such as myself is either "living in denial" of untamable homosexual desires or "was never gay" and thus beyond temptation. Since I have never experienced homosexual feelings or desires, the accusation that I am "living in denial" of my supposed homosexuality is demonstrably false. Unfortunately, many who have successfully left the gay lifestyle face the same cruel and baseless indictment, hurled by those who cannot bring themselves to accept that individuals can have victory over sexual depravity.

As for those who would argue that since I was never gay, my story cannot relate to those who were "born gay," I respond that the belief that people are "born gay" is an unsubstantiated theory that is questioned by many homosexuals themselves. It is more correct to state that, for numerous reasons that we only imperfectly understand, men and women *enter*, or become involved in, the gay lifestyle.

And there, but for the grace of God, I could have gone. Such is the weakness of the human frame that someone such as myself with deep personal needs for masculine affirmation could be seduced into experimenting with homosexuality. More important, the lesson of my story is that it is possible to resist the temptation to enter into the immoral homosexual lifestyle.

Yet Alec did "wound" me in a way that he surely did not intend: for many years after my experience with him I remained wary of men who showed interest in me as a person. Not that I necessarily suspected them of being homosexual; I just could not overcome the persistent, irrational fear that arose from my experience with Alec. Thus, he had the effect of aggravating my emotional wounds, leaving me even more insecure and unable to trust others. Alec's underlying motive, which was to have a sexual relationship with me, more than canceled out the encouragement he lavished upon me.

One might protest that I overreacted—that I should have "taken the good and discarded the rest." But I suspect those who have been used by others for ulterior motives will understand my reaction. Each of us—men and women alike—want to be accepted for who we are, not as sexual objects. And though we may be guilty of naiveté and may struggle to face the unpleasant truth, in the end we either recognize the counterfeit "love"—or pay a grievous emotional price. In the words of the biblical proverb, though the "lips of an adulteress drip honey, and her speech is smoother than oil, in the end she is bitter as gall."

Thankfully, the Lord knew how needy I was and had mercy upon me. Step by step, year by year, He worked out His wonderful plan for my life—a plan that I could never have imagined. And along the way He brought virtuous men of character across my path, who served as positive, fatherly role models.

My experience with Alec led eventually to the opportunity to engage the culture regarding the issue of homosexuality in my work at the Family Research Council. And I am thankful for Alec, for it is through knowing both the promise and the tragedy of his remarkable life that I can have genuine compassion for those who are trapped in the gay lifestyle. So even the "wounding" that Alec caused served a divine purpose in my life and is infinitely preferable to a "wound unto death." My prayer is that those who are suffering will also receive healing for the wounds caused by that dark obsession.

The Homosexuality Issue in Contemporary Churches and Denominations

REVISIONISTS CONTINUE their efforts to convince various church bodies to not only tolerate but also sanction homosexual behavior. In its report, "Mixed Blessings: Organized Religion and Gay and Lesbian Americans in 1998," the homosexual activist organization Human Rights Campaign (HRC) asserted that "there is no single religious view about gay and lesbian people. Nor is there one set of answers to the questions: Is gay and lesbian sex a sin? Should ministers and rabbis bless gay and lesbian unions?"[1]

The HRC report, however, provided little comfort to homosexuals demanding that their lifestyle be considered morally appropriate. After decades of concerted efforts by revisionists, the report found that not one of the eight largest Christian churches in America has given its ecclesiastical blessing to homosexuality.

The positions of some major denominations are provided below. Individual ministers, churches, and even denomination-sponsored organizations within each of the various church bodies seek the full acceptance of homosexual behavior. However, it is important to realize that such voices do not necessarily constitute the official position of the church or denomination.

The Roman Catholic Church

As with any large and multifaceted church body, isolated pronouncements by individual priests or church-related organizations are sometimes mistakenly viewed as the official position of Roman Catholics. That position, however, is unmistakable: although the Roman Catholic Church condemns prejudice toward homosexuals, it nonetheless maintains unequivocally that homosexual acts are always intrinsically evil. The official teaching of Roman Catholics was affirmed in 1975 by the Sacred Congregation for the Doctrine of the Faith in its "Declaration on Certain Questions Concerning Sexual Ethics." The declaration stated that homosexual actions are "condemned as a serious depravity" and "intrinsically disordered."[2]

In 1998 the National Conference of Catholic Bishops issued the statement "Always Our Children: A Pastoral Message to Parents of Homosexual Children and Suggestions for Pastoral Ministers." The pastoral statement noted that while "homosexual orientation" was in itself not considered sinful, it was nonetheless "objectively disordered." The Catholic Church maintains that through spiritual and psychological counseling, prayer, and the formation of Christian virtue, such individuals can live chaste lives and experience substantial healing from homosexual desires.

The Episcopal Church

The Episcopal Church's 1979 General Convention passed a resolution which stated, "There should be no barrier to the ordination of qualified persons of either heterosexual or homosexual orientation whose behavior the Church considers wholesome." However, the resolution further specified chastity as a qualification for ordination: "We believe it is not appropriate for this Church to ordain a practicing homosexual, or any person who is engaged in heterosexual relations outside of marriage."

In 2000 the Episcopal Church's General Convention endorsed a new policy acknowledging there are Episcopal couples, "acting in good conscience," in lifelong committed relationships outside marriage that should receive "prayerful support, encouragement and pastoral care." Revisionists applauded the measure, even though the measure stopped short of specifically mentioning homosexuals.

The Episcopal Church is a member of the worldwide Anglican Community. In 1998 the International Lambeth Conference of Anglican Bishops approved a resolution upholding "faithfulness in marriage between a man and a woman in lifelong union." The resolution, while "rejecting homosexual practice as incompatible with Scripture," calls on congregants "to minister pastorally and sensitively" to homosexuals. The resolution stated that it "cannot advise the legitimizing or blessing of same-sex union, nor the ordination of those involved in same-gender unions."[3]

The Southern Baptist Convention

The SBC, the largest Protestant denomination in the United States, is opposed to homosexuality and has passed numerous resolutions condemning homosexual behavior. In 1991 the SBC passed a resolution saying that homosexuality is "outside the will of God," and that "it is the responsibility and privilege of the church to minister to homosexuals." Responding to efforts to legalize homosexual marriage, in 1998 the SBC convention qualified its definition of "marriage" as "the uniting of one man and one woman."[4]

In 1998 the general board of another Baptist denomination, the American Baptist Churches in the U.S.A., adopted the recommendation of a unity committee that noncelibate homo-sexuality is "incompatible" with Christian teaching and the "prevailing understanding of American Baptists." In 1999, four American Baptist churches that welcomed noncelibate homo-sexuals lost an appeal before the general board and are no longer welcome in the denomination.

The United Methodist Church

The Book of Discipline of the United Methodist Church regu-lates the activities of the UMC worldwide. Regarding the issue of homosexuality, the *Book of Discipline* states, "Since the practice of homosexuality is incompatible with Christian teaching, self-avowed practicing homosexuals are not to be accepted as candi-dates, ordained as ministers or appointed to serve in The United Methodist Church."

At the 2000 General Conference, a resolution that would have required a loyalty oath of any minister assigned to a con-gregation failed to pass. The oath read, "I do not believe that homosexuality is God's perfect will for any person. I will not practice it. I will not promote it. I will not allow its promotion to be encouraged under my authority." However, by a 628 to 337 vote, the delegates passed a resolution reaffirming their belief that homosexual behavior is incompatible with Christian teaching.

The Presbyterian Church (U.S.A.)

In 1978 the General Assembly of the PCUSA formally wel-comed gays and lesbians as members. However, they are not eli-gible to be elevated to the level of elder, deacon, or minister. The Assembly stated that homosexuality was "not God's wish for humanity. . . . Even where the homosexual orientation has not been consciously sought or chosen, it is neither a gift from God nor a state nor a condition like race; it is a result of our living in a fallen world."

In 1996 delegates passed an amendment requiring "all Presbyterian ministers, deacons, and elders to be married and faithful or single and celibate." In 2000 the General Assembly narrowly approved a ban on same-sex ceremonies. However, the measure failed to gain the required two-thirds approval by a majority of the church's 173 regional units to become part of the Book of Order.

The Assemblies of God

In 1979 the General Presbytery of the Assemblies of God, the world's largest Pentecostal denomination, adopted a report on homosexuality. The position paper rejected demands for equality by homosexual activists and stated that homosexuality represented the "alarming erosion of national moral standards." Homosexual behavior is described as a sin against God and man.

When ministering to homosexuals, the report issued the following caution: "Believers must trust the Holy Spirit to guide them in distinguishing between those who honestly want God's salvation and those who may be recruiting sympathizers for homosexuality as an alternate lifestyle."

Notes

Introduction

1. At the request of "Alec's" widow, I have changed the name and certain personal details of the man whose story is told in this book.

Chapter 1

1. "Homosexuality and Hope: Statement of the Catholic Medical Association" (Catholic Medical Association: 2001): 4–7.

Chapter 4

1. Lisa Bennett, "Mixed Blessings: Organized Religion and Gay and Lesbian Americans in 1998," Human Rights Campaign Foundation (1998): 7.

2. Derrick Sherwin Bailey, *Homosexuality and the Western Christian Tradition* (London: Longmans, Green, & Co., 1955).

3. Ibid., 4.

4. Peter J. Gomes, *The Good Book: Reading the Bible with Mind and Heart* (New York: William Morrow & Co., Inc., 1996), 152.

5. Robin Scroggs, *The New Testament and Homosexuality* (Philadelphia: Fortress Press, 1983), 73.

6. Bailey, *Homosexuality,* 55.

7. Ibid., 54. Bailey admits that *nebalah* "often relates to sexual offences" and lists numerous references that support the sexual interpretation of the term.

8. Harold I. Haas, "Homosexuality," *Currents in Theology and Missions* 5 (April 1978): 97.

9. David L. Bartlett, "A Biblical Perspective on Homosexuality," in *Homosexuality and the Christian Faith: A Symposium,* ed. Harold L. Twiss (Valley Forge: Judson Press, 1978), 25.

10. James Nelson, "Homosexuality and the Church," *Christianity and Crisis* 37 (1977): 64.

11. That *qadesh* refers to homosexual and not heterosexual prostitution is indicated by the rendering of the word in the Septuagint (LXX), the Greek translation of the Hebrew Bible dating to around 150 B.C. In 1 Kings 22:46, *qadesh* is translated by the Greek word *endiellagmenos* ("one who has changed his nature"). Bailey states that "the *endiellagmenos* may be either one who has altered his nature by becoming a homosexual pervert, or one who has been transformed by apostasy from a worshiper of Yahweh into a servant of idols" (*Homosexuality and the Western Christian Tradition,* 151). Revisionists ignore, however, that the two possibilities are not mutually exclusive and are in fact intrinsically connected. Israel's adoption of Canaanite idolatry entailed both spiritual and moral apostasy.

12. Bailey, *Homosexuality,* 30.

13. P. Michael Ukleja, "Homosexuality and the Old Testament," *Bibliotheca Sacra* 140 (July–September 1983): 259.

14. S. R. Driver, *A Critical and Exegetical Commentary on Deuteronomy* (Edinburgh: T & T Clark, 1895), 265.

15. See Tom Horner, *Jonathan Loved David: Homosexuality in Biblical Times* (Philadelphia: Westminster Press, 1978).

16. Anton N. Marco, "'Gay Theology' and 'Gay Rights': 'Biblical Bedfellows' or Unholy Alliance?" *Social Justice Review* 87 (March–April 1996): 39.

17. Scroggs, *The New Testament,* 71.

18. Ibid., 128.

19. Anthony Campolo, "A Christian Sociologist Looks at Homosexuality," *Wittenburg Door* 39 (11 October 1977): 17.

20. Ibid.

21. Scroggs, *The New Testament,* 115.

22. Philo, *The Contemplative Life,* 59.

23. Bennett J. Sims, "Sex and Homosexuality," *Christianity Today* 22 (24 February 1978): 25.

24. John Boswell, *Christianity, Social Tolerance, and Homosexuality* (Chicago: University of Chicago Press, 1980), 344.

25. Scroggs, *The New Testament,* 108.

26. Boswell, *Christianity,* 340.

27. Scroggs, *The New Testament,* 65.

28. William F. Arndt and F. Wilbur Gingrich, *A Greek-English Lexicon of the New Testament and Other Early Christian Literature,* 2d. ed. (Chicago: The University of Chicago Press, 1979), 115.

29. No lexicon could be found dissenting from the identification of *arsenokoitai* with homosexuality. See Colin Brown, ed., *The New International Dictionary of New Testament Theology,* vol. 2 (Grand Rapids: Zondervan, 1976), 569–70; G. W. H. Lampe, *A Patristic Greek Lexicon* (Oxford University Press, 1961), 230–31; Henry George Liddell and Robert Scott, *A Greek-English Lexicon,* 8th ed. (New York: American Book Company, 1897), 223; E. A. Sophocles, *Greek Lexicon of the Roman and Byzantine Periods,* vol. 1 (New York: Frederick Ungar Publishing Co., 1887), 253. There is no reference to *arsenokoitai* in the *Theological Dictionary of the New Testament,* ed., Gerhard Griedrich (Grand Rapids: Eerdmans, 1978).

30. Boswell, *Christianity,* 340.

31. Scroggs, *The New Testament,* 64.

32. Aristotle, *Problems* 4.26. Compare *Lucian* 37.

33. *Roman Antiquities*; trans. From Boswell, *Christianity*, 339. Boswell obviously prefers the other possible definition given by Dionysius: someone who is "gentle by nature and unruffled (*malakos*) by anger, as others claim." The point here is that passive homosexual behavior is a legitimate definition of the term *malakos,* which Boswell denies—despite the fact that we have quoted his own translation of Dionysius.

34. Robert A. J. Gagnon, *The Bible and Homosexual Practice* (Nashville: Abingdon Press, 2000), 309.

35. Bartlett, "A Biblical Perspective on Homosexuality," 25.

36. Arndt-Gingrich, *A Greek-English Lexicon,* 488.

37. D. Hans Leitzmann, *An Die Korinther I—II* (Tubingen: J. C. B. Mohr, 1969), 27.

38. John von Rohr, "Toward a Theology of Homosexuality," in *Is Gay Good? Ethics, Theology, and Homosexuality,* W. D. Oberholtzer ed. (London: SCM, 1967), 76.

39. Thomas Maurer, "Toward a Theology of Homosexuality: Tried and Found Trite and Tragic," in *Is Gay Good? Ethics, Theology, and Homosexuality,* W. D. Oberholtzer ed. (London: SCM, 1967), 76.

Chapter 5

1. Anthony Kosnik, chairperson et al., *Human Sexuality: New Directions in American Catholic Thought* (Garden City, New York: Doubleday, 1979).

2. Ibid., 23. For a critique of this study see William E. May and John F. Harvey, "On Understanding Human Sexuality: a Critique of the CTSA Study," *Communio* 4 (fall 1977): 195–225.

3. David L. Bartlett, "Biblical Perspectives on Homosexuality," *Foundations* 20 (April–June 1977): 26.

4. Mark Olson, "Untangling the Web," *The Other Side* 20 (April 1984): 25.

5. Walter C. Kaiser, "Leviticus 18:5 and Paul: Do This and You Shall Live (Eternally)," *Journal of the Evangelical Theological Society* 14 (winter 1971): 26.

6. Anthony Phillips, *Ancient Israel's Criminal Law* (New York: Schocken Books, 1970), 125.

7. *The New Bible Dictionary*, ed. J. D. Douglas (Grand Rapids: Eerdmans, 1962), s.v. "Law," by J. Murray.

8. Kosnik, *Human Sexuality*, 23–24.

9. James Nelson, "Homosexuality and the Church," *Christianity and Crisis* 37 (1977): 64.

10. Thielicke, Helmut, *The Ethics of Sex*, translated by John Doberstein (New York: Harper & Row, 1964), 284.

11. K. J. Dover, *Greek Homosexuality* (Cambridge, Mass.: Harvard University Press, 1978), 144.

12. Plato, *Symposium*, 191e.

13. Boswell, *Christianity*, 49–50.

14. Philo, *De Specialibus Legibus*, 3.37–42.

15. Josephus, *Contra Apion*, II.273–75.

16. Clement of Alexandria, *Miscellanies*, 3:1. Clement may simply have been referring to those who, for whatever reason, have no interest in marriage. However, the reference to those experiencing a "natural aversion to a woman" may also suggest homosexual feelings.

17. Boswell, *Christianity*, 109.

18. Walter Wink, "Biblical Perspectives on Homosexuality," *Christian Century* 96 (7 November 1979): 1085.

19. Lisa Sowle Cahill, "Sexual Issues in Christian Theological Ethics: A Review of Recent Studies," *Religious Studies Review* 4 (January 1978): 13.

20. Charles E. Curran, "Homosexuality and Moral Theology: Methodological and Substantive Considerations," in Edward Batchelor, ed., *Homosexuality and Ethics* (New York: Pilgrim, 1980), 93.

21. See Yvette Cantu, "The Gay Gene: Going, Going, Gone" *Insight* (Washington, D.C.: Family Research Council, 2000).

22. Ed Stein, *The Mismeasure of Desire: The Science, Theory, and Ethics of Sexual Orientation* (New York: Oxford University Press, 1999).

Chapter 6

1. Kosnik, *Human Sexuality,* 112ff.

2. Roger Shinn, "Homosexuality: Christian Conviction and Inquiry," in *Homosexuality and Ethics,* ed. Edward Batchelor Jr. (New York: Pilgrim Press, 1980), 11.

3. John J. McNeil, *The Church and the Homosexual* (Kansas City: Sheed, Andrews and McMeel, 1976), 65.

4. Oberholtzer, *Is Gay Good?,* 52.

5. Austin Flannery, ed., *Vatican Council II: More Postconciliar Documents* (Northport, N.Y.: Costello Publishing Co., 1979), 508.

6. William Muehl, "Some Words of Caution," in *Homosexuality and Ethics,* ed. Edward Batchelor Jr. (New York: Pilgrim Press, 1980), 76.

7. Flannery, *Vatican Council II,* 508.

8. Letha Scanzoni, "Putting a Face on Homosexuality," *Other Side* 14 (June 1978): 9–10.

9. John Alexander, "Homosexuality: It's Not that Clear," *Other Side* 14 (June 1978): 213.

10. D. J. Atkinson, *Homosexuals in the Church* (Grand Rapids: Eerdmans, 1979), 69–70.

11. Gerhard Von Rad, *Genesis: A Commentary* (Philadelphia: Westminster Press, 1961), 58.

12. Raymond F. Collins, "The Bible and Sexuality," *Biblical Theology Bulletin* 7 (October 1977): 156.

13. Donald J. Keefe, "Biblical Symbolism and the Morality of *In Vitro* Fertilization," *Theology Digest* 22 (winter 1974): 316.

14. Hershal J. Matt, "Sin, Crime, Sickness or Alternative Life Style?: A Jewish Approach to Homosexuality," *Judaism* 27 (winter 1978): 14–15.

15. Troy Perry, *Don't Be Afraid Anymore* (New York: St. Martin's Press, 1990), 40.

16. William E. May and John F. Harvey, "On Understanding Human Sexuality: A Critique of the CTSA Study," *Communio* 4 (fall 1977): 216.

17. John T. Noonan Jr., "Genital Good," *Communio* 8 (fall 1981): 220.

18. Ibid.

Chapter 7

1. Richard John Neuhaus, "In the Case of John Boswell," *First Things* (March 1994): 56.

2. Ralph Blair, *Review: A Quarterly of Evangelicals Concerned* 5 (fall 1980): 1.

3. Neuhaus, "In the Case of John Boswell," 56.

4. Glenn W. Olsen, "The Gay Middle Ages: A Response to Professor Boswell," *Communio* 8 (summer 1981): 127.

5. Ibid., 131–32.

6. Ibid., 133.

7. John C. Moore, "Reviews of books," *American Historical Review* 86 (April 1981): 381.

8. John Boswell, *Same-Sex Unions in Premodern Europe* (New York: Villard Books, 1994).

9. Brent D. Shaw, "A Groom of One's Own?" *New Republic* (July 18–25, 1994): 35.

10. Ibid.

11. Robin Darling Young, "Gay Marriage: Reimagining Church History," *First Things* (November 1994): 43–48.

12. Shaw, "A Groom of One's Own?", 36.

13. Young, "Gay Marriage," 43–48.

14. Shinn, "Homosexuality," 9.

15. *Didache or Teachings of the Twelve Apostles,* cap. II, vol. 7; and *Epistle of Barnabas,* cap. XIX, vol. 1, *The Anti Nicene Fathers,* eds. Alexander Roberts and James Donaldson (Grand Rapids: Eerdmans, 1966).

16. Quoted in Bailey, *Homosexuality,* 25.

17. St. Basil, *De Renuntiatione Saeculi,* trans. M. Monica Wagner, vol. 9 *The Fathers of the Church* (Washington, D.C.: Catholic University of America, 1948).

18. Bailey, *Homosexuality,* 89.

19. Clement, *Paedagogos* 2.10.86–87, 3.3.21.3.

20. Ibid.

21. St. Augustine, *Confessions,* III, viii, trans. Rex Warner (New York: New American).

22. *The Theodosian Code,* trans. Clyde Pharr (Princeton, N.J.: Princeton University Press, 1952), 231–32.

23. *Institutes,* IV, xviii, 4, trans. J. B. Moyle (Oxford: Clarendon Press, 1937).

24. Quoted in Bailey, *Homosexuality,* 73–74.

25. Thomas Aquinas, *Summa Theologica,* II:2, question 154:12, trans. Fathers of the English Dominican Province (New York: Benziger Brothers, 1947), 1826.

26. Martin Luther, *Luther's Works,* ed. Jaroslav Pelican, *Lectures on Genesis,* (St. Louis: Concordia House, 1961), 254.

27. John Calvin, *Commentary on I Corinthians,* trans. John W. Fraser (Grand Rapids: Eerdmans, 1960), 124.

28. Cf. Heidelberg Catechism, II, Question 87; Augsburg Confession, II.2; Westminster Confession, cap. 24.

29. Karl Barth, *Church Dogmatics,* trans. G. T. Thomson and Harold Knight, III.4 (Edinburgh: T & T Clark, 1961), 162.

30. J. D. Unwin, *Sexual Regulations and Cultural Behavior* (Trona, Calif.: Frank M. Darrow, 1934), 5.

31. Ibid., 20, 32.

32. Ibid., 17, 20–21.

33. Muehl, "Some Words of Caution," 190.

Chapter 8

1. Bill Roundy, "STD Rates on the Rise," *New York Blade News* (15 December 2000): 1.

2. Bill Roundy, "STDs Up among Gay Men: CDC Says Rise Is Due to HIV Misperceptions," *Washington Blade* (8 December 2000).

3. Richard A. Zmuda, "Rising Rates of Anal Cancer for Gay Men," *Cancer News* (17 August 2000).

4. *Mortality and Morbidity Weekly Report, Centers for Disease Control and Prevention* (4 September 1998): 708.

5. "Viral Hepatitis B—Frequently Asked Questions," *Centers for Disease Control and Prevention* (29 September 2000), <http://www.cdc.gov/ncidod/diseases/hepatitis/b/faqb.htm>.

6. "Hepatitis C: Epidemiology: Transmission Modes," Centers for Disease Control and Prevention, (1998), <http://www.cdc.gov/ncidod/diseases/hepatitis/c>.

7. "Gonorrhea," Centers for Disease Control and Prevention: Division of Sexually Transmitted Diseases (September 2000), <http://www.cdc.gov/nchstp/dstd/Fact_Sheets/FactsGonorrhea. htm>.

8. *Mortality and Morbidity Weekly Report, Centers for Disease Control and Prevention* (29 January 1999): 48.

9. J. Vincelette, J. G. Baril, R. Allard, "Predicators of Chlamydial Infection and Gonorrhea among Patients Seen by Private Practitioners," *Canadian Medical Association Journal* 144 (1995): 713–21.

10. SPR Jebakumar, C. Storey, J. Nelson, B. Goorney, K. R. Haye, "Value of Screening for Oropharyngeal Chlamydia Trachomatis Infection," *Journal of Clinical Pathology* 48 (1995): 658–61.

11. "Some Facts about Syphilis," *Centers for Disease Control and Prevention: Division of Sexually Transmitted Diseases* (October

1999),<http://www.cdc.gov/nchstp/dstd/Fact_Sheets/ Syphilis_Facts.htm>.

12. C. M. Hutchinson, A. M. Rompalo, M. T. Reichart, E. W. Hook, "Characteristics of Patients with Syphilis Attending Baltimore STD Clinics," *Archives of Internal Medicine* 151 (1991): 511–16.

13. "Syphilis Elimination: History in the Making," *Centers for Disease Control and Prevention: Division of Sexually Transmitted Diseases* (May 2001), <http://www.cdc.gov/nchstp/ dstd/Fact_Sheets/Syphilis_Facts.htm>.

14. Homosexual advocates object to the use of this term, which they say unfairly stigmatizes homosexual behavior. See *Health Implications Associated with Homosexuality* (Austin: The Medical Institute for Sexual Health, 1999), 55.

15. "STD Treatment Guidelines: Proctitis, Proctocolitis, and Enteritis," JAMA Women's Health, 1993, <http://www.ama-assn.org/special/std/treatmnt/guide/stdg3470.htm>.

16. Jack Morin, *Anal Pleasure and Health: A Guide for Men and Women* (San Francisco: Down There Press, 1998), 220.

17. *Health Implications,* 56.

18. Ibid., "STD Treatment Guidelines."

19. Ibid., *Health Implications*; see Morin, *Anal Pleasure and Health,* 220–21.

20. Ibid., *Health Implications.*

21. "Table 5. AIDS cases by age group, exposure category, and sex, reported through December 2001, United States," *Centers for Disease Control and Prevention: Division of HIV/AIDS Prevention* (24 September 2002), <http://www.cdc.gov/ hiv/stats/hasr1302/table5.htm>.

22. "Studies Point to Increased Risks of Anal Cancer," *Washington Blade* (2 June 2000), <http://www.washblade.com/ health/000602hm.htm>.

23. Ulysses Torassa, "Some with HIV Aren't Disclosing before Sex; UCSF Researcher's 1,397-Person Study Presented

during AIDS Conference," *San Francisco Examiner* (15 July 2000), A1.

24. Jon Garbo, "Gay and Bi Men Less Likely to Disclose They Have HIV," *GayHealth News* (18 July 2000), <http://www.gayhealth.com/templates/0/news?record=136>.

25. Ibid.

26. "Young People at Risk: HIV/AIDS among America's Youth," *Centers for Disease Control and Prevention: Divisions of HIV/AIDS Prevention* (11 March 2002), <http://www.cdc.gov/hiv/pubs/facts/youth.htm>. Original emphasis.

27. Ibid.

28. "Need for Sustained HIV Prevention Among Men Who Have Sex with Men," *Centers for Disease Control: Divisions of HIV/AIDS Prevention* (11 March 2002), <http://www.cdc.gov/hiv/pubs/facts/msm.htm>.

29. Resurgent Bacterial Sexually Transmitted Disease among Men Who Have Sex with Men—King County, Washington, 1997–99, *Centers for Disease Control and Prevention, Morbidity and Mortality Weekly Report* (September 10, 1999): 773–77.

30. Ibid. Cp. "Scientists know that the likelihood of both acquiring and spreading HIV is two to five times greater in people with STDs" ("Need for Sustained HIV Prevention," Ibid.)

31. Bob Roehr, "Anal Cancer and You," *Between the Lines News* (16 November 2000).

32. Ibid., "Studies Point to Increased Risks of Anal Cancer."

33. Rhonda Smith, "HPV Can Be Transmitted between Women," *Washington Blade* (4 December 1998), 18.

34. Ibid., 352.

35. Ibid., 350.

36. V. Gonzales et al., "Sexual and Drug-Use Risk Factors for HIV and STDs: A Comparison of Women with and without Bisexual Experiences," *American Journal of Public Health* 89 (December 1999): 1846.

37. "Bisexuals Serve as 'Bridge' Infecting Women with HIV," *Reuters News Service* (30 July 2000).

38. Katherine Fethers, Caron Marks, Adrian Mindel, and Claudia S. Estcourt, "Sexually Transmitted Infections and Risk Behaviors in Women Who Have Sex with Women," *Sexually Transmitted Infections* 76 (July 2000): 345.

39. Rhonda Smith, "Childbirth Linked with Smaller Breast Tumor Size," *Washington Blade* (17 December 1999), 21.

40. Rhonda Smith, "HPV can be Transmitted between Women," *Washington Blade* (4 December 1998), 18.

41. Fethers, "Sexually Transmitted Infections," 345.

42. Joanne Hall, "Lesbians Recovering from Alcoholic Problems: An Ethnographic Study of Health Care Expectations," *Nursing Research* 43 (1994): 238–44.

43. Peter Freiberg, "Study: Alcohol Use More Prevalent for Lesbians," *Washington Blade* (12 January 2001): 21.

44. Karen Paige Erickson, Karen F. Trocki, "Sex, Alcohol and Sexually Transmitted Diseases: A National Survey," *Family Planning Perspectives* 26 (December 1994): 261.

45. Lettie L. Lockhart et al., "Letting out the Secret: Violence in Lesbian Relationships," *Journal of Interpersonal Violence* 9 (December 1994): 469–92.

46. Gwat Yong Lie and Sabrina Gentlewarrier, "Intimate Violence in Lesbian Relationships: Discussion of Survey Findings and Practice Implications," *Journal of Social Service Research* 15 (1991): 41–59.

47. D. Island and P. Letellier, *Men Who Beat the Men Who Love Them: Battered Gay Men and Domestic Violence* (New York: Haworth Press, 1991), 14.

48. "Violence Between Intimates," *Bureau of Justice Statistics Selected Findings* (November 1994): 2.

49. *Health Implications,* 79.

50. J. Bradford et al., "National Lesbian Health Care Survey: Implications for Mental Health Care," *Journal of Consulting and*

Clinical Psychology 62 (1994): 239, cited in *Health Implications Associated with Homosexuality,* 81.

51. R. Herrell et al., "A Co-twin Study in Adult Men," *Archives of General Psychiatry* 56 (1999): 867–74.

52. D. Fergusson et al., "Is Sexual Orientation Related to Mental Health Problems and Suicidality in Young People?" *Archives of General Psychiatry* 56 (October 1999), 876–84.

53. Ibid., 880.

54. Robert S. Hogg et al., "Modeling the Impact of HIV Disease on Mortality in Gay and Bisexual Men," *International Journal of Epidemiology* 26 (1997): 657.

55. Quoted in Gabriel Rotello, *Sexual Ecology: AIDS and the Destiny of Gay Men* (New York: Penguin Books, 1997): 286.

Chapter 9

1. Marilyn Elias, "Growing Up with Gay Parents: We are Family, Too, Children Say," *USA Today,* 23 August 2001, D1.

2. "PCT 14: Unmarried-Partner Households by Sex of Partners" (U.S. Census Bureau: Census 2000 Summary File 1). Available at www.census.gov.

3. Dan Black et al., "Demographics of the Gay and Lesbian Population in the United States: Evidence from Available Systematic Data Sources," *Demography* 37 (May 2000): 150.

4. Ellen C. Perrin, M.D., and the Committee on Psychosocial Aspects of Child and Family Health, American Academy of Pediatrics, "Technical Report: Coparent or Second-Parent Adoption by Same-Sex Parents," *Pediatrics* 109, no. 2 (February 2002): 343.

5. P. A. Belcastro et al., "A Review of Data-Based Studies Addressing the Affects of Homosexual Parenting on Children's Sexual and Social Functioning," *Journal of Divorce and Remarriage* 20 (1993): 105, 106.

6. J. M. Bailey et al., "Sexual Orientation of Adult Sons of Gay Fathers," *Developmental Psychology* 31 (1995): 124.

7. Jerry J. Bigner and R. Brooke Jacobson, "Adult Responses to Child Behavior and Attitudes Toward Fathering: Gay and Nongay Fathers," *Journal of Homosexuality* 23 (1992): 99–112.

8. Charlotte J. Patterson, "Families of the Lesbian Baby Boom: Parent's Division of Labor and Children's Adjustment," *Development Psychology* 31 (1995): 122.

9. Richard Green et al., "Lesbian Mothers and Their Children: A Comparison with Solo Parent Heterosexual Mothers and Their Children," *Archives of Sexual Behavior* 15 (1986): 167–84.

10. Laura Lott-Whitehead and Carol T. Tully, "The Family Lives of Lesbian Mothers," *Smith College Studies in Social Work* 63 (1993): 265.

11. Golombok et al., "Children in Lesbian and Single-Parent Households: Psychosexual and Psychiatric Appraisal," *Journal of Child Psychology and Psychiatry* 24 (1983): 569.

12. Mary B. Harris and Pauline H. Turner, "Gay and Lesbian Parents," *Journal of Homosexuality* 12 (1985): 104.

13. Ibid., 112.

14. Nanette Gartrell et al., "The National Lesbian Family Study: Interviews with Prospective Mothers," *American Journal of Orthopsychiatry* 66 (1996): 279.

15. A. P. Bell and M. S. Weinberg, *Homosexualities: A Study of Diversity Among Men and Women* (New York: Simon and Schuster, 1978), 308, 309; see also A. P. Bell, M. S. Weinberg, and S. K. Hammersmith, *Sexual Preference* (Bloomington: Indiana University Press, 1981).

16. Paul Van de Ven et al., "A Comparative Demographic and Sexual Profile of Older Homosexually Active Men," *Journal of Sex Research* 34 (1997): 354.

17. David P. McWhirter and Andrew M. Mattison, *The Male Couple: How Relationships Develop* (Englewood Cliffs: Prentice-Hall, 1984), 252, 253.

18. M. Saghir and E. Robins, *Male and Female Homosexuality* (Baltimore: Williams & Wilkins, 1973), 225; see also L. A. Peplau and H. Amaro, "Understanding Lesbian Relationships," in *Homosexuality: Social, Psychological, and Biological Issues,* ed. J. Weinrich and W. Paul (Beverly Hills: Sage, 1982).

19. Robert T. Michael et al., *Sex in America: A Definitive Survey* (Boston: Little, Brown & Company, 1994), 105.

20. Michael W. Wiederman, "Extramarital Sex: Prevalence and Correlates in a National Survey," *Journal of Sex Research* 34 (1997): 170.

21. A. M. Johnson et al., "Sexual Lifestyles and HIV Risk," *Nature* 360 (1992): 410–12; see also R. Turner, "Landmark French and British Studies Examine Sexual Behavior, Including Multiple Partners, Homosexuality," *Family Planning Perspectives* 25 (1993): 91, 92.

22. F. Tasker and S. Golombok, "Adults Raised as Children in Lesbian Families," *American Journal of Orthopsychiatry* 65 (April 1995): 213.

23. ACSF Investigators, "AIDS and Sexual Behavior in France," *Nature* 360 (1992): 407–409; J. M. Bailey et al., "Sexual Orientation of Adult Sons of Gay Fathers," *Developmental Psychology* 31 (1995): 124–29; John O. G. Billy et al., "The Sexual Behavior of Men in the United States," *Family Planning Perspectives* 25 (1993): 52–60; A. M. Johnson et al., "Sexual Lifestyles and HIV Risk," *Nature* 360 (1992): 410–12.

24. Judith Stacey and Timothy J. Biblarz, "(How) Does the Sexual Orientation of Parents Matter," *American Sociological Review* 66 (2001): 174, 179.

25. F. Tasker and S. Golombok, "Do Parents Influence the Sexual Orientation of Children?" *Developmental Psychology* 32 (1996): 7.

26. Judith Stacey and Timothy J. Biblarz, "(How) Does the Sexual Orientation of Parents Matter," *American Sociological Review* 66 (2001): 174, 179.

27. P. Cameron and K. Cameron, "Homosexual Parents," *Adolescence* 31 (1996): 772.

28. Children raised by single parents are more likely to live in poverty, fail in school, abuse alcohol and other substances, engage in criminal behavior, and be victims of child abuse. See *Why Marriage Matters: Twenty-One Conclusions from the Social Sciences* (New York: Institute for American Values, 2002), 9, 10, 12–13, 15–16, 17.

29. Paula Ettelbrick, quoted in William B. Rubenstein, "Since When Is Marriage a Path to Liberation?" *Lesbians, Gay Men, and the Law* (New York: The New Press, 1993), 398, 400.

30. Mary Mendola, *The Mendola Report* (New York: Crown, 1980), 53.

31. L. Koepke et al., "Relationship Quality in a Sample of Lesbian Couples with Children and Child-free Lesbian Couples," *Family Relations* 41 (1992): 228.

32. J. J. Bigner and R. B. Jacobson, "Adult Responses to Child Behavior and Attitudes Toward Fathering," Frederick W. Bozett, ed., *Homosexuality and the Family* (New York: Harrington Park Press, 1989), 174, 175.

Chapter 10

1. Dawn Fisher, "Adult Sex Offenders: Who are They? Why and How Do They Do It?" in Tony Morrison et al., eds., *Sexual Offending Against Children* (London: Routledge, 1994), 11.

2. John Briere et al., eds., *The APSAC Handbook on Child Maltreatment* (Thousand Oaks, California: Sage Publications, 1996), 52, 53.

3. Bill Watkins and Arnon Bentovim, "The Sexual Abuse of Male Children and Adolescents: A Review of Current Research," *Journal of Child Psychiatry* 33 (1992); in Byrgen Finkelman, *Sexual Abuse* (New York: Garland Publishing, 1995), 300.

4. Kurt Freund et al., "Pedophilia and Heterosexuality vs. Homosexuality," *Journal of Sex & Marital Therapy* 10 (1984):

197. "The proportional prevalence of offenders against male children in this group of 457 offenders against children was 36 percent." See also, Kurt Freund et al., "Heterosexuality, Homosexuality, and Erotic Age Preference," *Journal of Sex Research* 26 (1989): 107. "Approximately one-third of these individuals had victimized boys and two-thirds had victimized girls. This finding is consistent with the proportions reported in two earlier studies."

5. Dan Black et al., "Demographics of the Gay and Lesbian Population in the United States: Evidence from Available Systematic Data Sources," *Demography* 37 (May 2000): 141.

6. John O. G. Billy et al., "The Sexual Behavior of Men in the United States," *Family Planning Perspectives* 25 (March/April 1993): 58.

7. Freund, "Heterosexuality, Homosexuality, and Erotic Age Preference," 107. In this and previous studies, Freund claims that homosexuals are no more likely than heterosexuals to be attracted to children (p. 115). However, Silverthorne et al., mentions the limitations of studies by Freund and others: "Studies of homosexual male preferences are also limited. . . . The Freund et al. (1973) study was possibly compromised because the homosexual men used in the study were selected to be sexually attracted to adults, but not teenaged males. The Bailey et al. (1994) study was limited in that it did not present participants with objective stimuli but simply asked participants to report what age of sexual partner they preferred . . . the Jankowiak et al. (1992) study . . . was limited in two ways: the homosexual male participants had a limited age range of 'middle-aged professionals' and the stimuli presented to participants were also of a limited age range ('university to middle-aged')." Silverthorne attempted to correct these deficiencies, and in his study found that homosexuals "preferred younger partners than those who preferred female partners"— including those as young as fifteen. Zebulon A. Silverthorne & Vernon L. Quinsey, "Sexual Partner Age Preferences of

Homosexual and Heterosexual Men and Women," *Archives of Sexual Behavior* 29 (February 2000): 67–76.

8. Ray Blanchard et al., "Fraternal Birth Order and Sexual Orientation in Pedophiles," *Archives of Sexual Behavior* 29 (2000): 464 (italics mine).

9. "[Pedophiles] can be of either sex or any [sexual] orientation, i.e., homosexual, heterosexual or bisexual." *Paedophilia: Some Questions and Answers* (London: Paedophilic Informational Exchange, 1978); quoted in Seth L. Goldstein, "Investigating Child Sexual Exploitation: Law Enforcement's Role," *FBI Law Enforcement Bulletin* 53 (January 1984): 23.

10. Scientific journals such as *Behavior Research and Therapy, Child Abuse and Neglect,* the *International Journal of Offender Therapy and Comparative Criminology,* the *Journal of Sex & Marital Therapy,* and the *Psychiatric Journal of the University of Ottawa* employ terms such as *homosexual pedophile, homosexual molestation,* etc. See Timothy J. Dailey, "Homosexuality and Child Sexual Abuse" (Family Research Council *Insight,* 2002): 5–7.

11. Kristin A. Danni et al., "An Analysis of Predicators of Child Sex Offender Types Using Presentence Investigation Reports," *International Journal of Offender Therapy and Comparative Criminology* 44 (2000): 491.

12. Silverthorne and Quinsey, "Sexual Partner Age Preferences," 73.

13. Karla Jay and Allen Young, *The Gay Report: Lesbians and Gay Men Speak Out about Sexual Experiences and Lifestyles* (New York: Summit Books, 1979), 275.

14. W. L. Marshall et. al., "Sexual Offenders against Male Children: Sexual Preferences," *Behavior Research and Therapy* 26 (March 1988): 383.

15. W. L. Marshall et al., "Early Onset and Deviant Sexuality in Child Molesters," *Journal of Interpersonal Violence* 6 (1991): 323–36.

16. W. D. Erickson, "Behavior Patterns of Child Molesters," *Archives of Sexual Behavior* 17 (1988): 83.

17. Michele Elliott, "Child Sexual Abuse Prevention: What Offenders Tell Us," *Child Abuse and Neglect* 19 (1995): 581.

18. Marshall, "Sexual Offenders against Male Children: Sexual Preferences," 383.

19. John M. W. Bradford et. al., "The Heterogeneity/ Homogeneity of Pedophilia," *Psychiatric Journal of the University of Ottawa* 13 (1988): 219.

20. Ibid., 253.

21. Ibid., 266.

22. George Archibald, "U.N. Group Keeps Ban on Gay Lobby" *Washington Times* (1 May 2002), A8.

23. Raymond-Jean Frontain, "The Works of Allen Ginsberg," *Journal of Homosexuality* 34 (1997): 109.

24. Mary Eberstadt, "'Pedophilia Chic' Reconsidered," *Weekly Standard* 6 (8 January 2001), 18–25.

25. Ibid., 21.

26. Ibid.

27. Ibid.

28. Ibid., 23.

29. Ibid. Emphasis added by Eberstadt.

30. Ibid., 23.

31. Ibid.

32. See the Gay Men's Press Web site at <http:www.gmp-pubs.co.uk/cgi-bin/web_store/web_store.cgi>.

33. Tom O'Carroll, *Paedophilia: The Radical Case* (Boston: Alyson Publications, 1982).

34. Daniel Tsang, ed., *The Age Taboo: Gay Male Sexuality, Power, and Consent* (Boston: Alyson Publications, 1981), 144.

35. Paula Martinac, "Mixed Messages on Pedophilia Need to be Clarified, Unified," *Washington Blade* (15 March 2002).

36. Ibid.

37. Marie E. Tomeo et al., "Comparative Data of Childhood and Adolescence Molestation in Heterosexual and Homosexual Persons," *Archives of Sexual Behavior* 30 (2001): 539.

38. Harry W. Haverkos et al., "The Initiation of Male Homosexual Behavior," *The Journal of the American Medical Association* 262 (28 July 1989): 501.

39. Watkins and Bentovim, "The Sexual Abuse of Male Children," 316.

Chapter 11

1. D. H. Hamer et al., "A Linkage Between DNA Markers on the X Chromosome and Male Sexual Orientation," *Science* 261 (1993): 321–27.

2. Ibid.

3. Ibid.

4. George Rice et al., "Male Homosexuality: Absence of Linkage to Microsatellite Markers at Xq28," *Science* 284 (April 1999): 665–67.

5. Ibid.

6. William Byne and Bruce Parsons, "Human Sexual Orientation: The Biologic Theories Reappraised," *Archives of General Psychiatry* 50 (March 1993): 228–39.

7. J. Michael Bailey, Richard C. Pillard, Michael C. Neale, and Yvonne Agyei, "Heritable Factors Influence Sexual Orientation in Women," *Archives of General Psychiatry* 50 (March 1993): 217–23.

8. Simon LeVay, "A Difference in Hypothalamic Structure Between Heterosexual and Homosexual Men," *Science* 258 (1991): 1034–37.

9. Dean Hamer and Peter Copeland, *Living with Our Genes: Why They Matter More Than You Think* (New York: Bantam Doubleday Dell, 1998), 188–89.

10. Ibid., 189.

11. Angela M. L. Pattatucci and Dean H. Hamer, "Development and Familiarity of Sexual Orientation in Females," *Behavior Genetics* 25 (1995): 407–19, cited in Hamer, ibid., 191.

12. Hamer, ibid.

13. Edward Stein, *The Mismeasure of Desire: The Science, Theory, and Ethics of Sexual Orientation* (New York: Oxford University Press, 1999).

14. Michael Bronski, "Blinded by Science," *The Advocate* (1 February 2000), 64.

15. Stein, *The Mismeasure of Desire,* 221.

16. David Perlman, "Brain Cell Study Finds Link to Homosexuality Tissue Differs Between Gay and Straight Men," *San Francisco Chronicle,* 30 August 1991, p. A1.

17. Stein, *The Mismeasure of Desire,* 215.

18. Bronski, "Blinded by Science," 64.

19. Neil and Briar Whitehead, *My Genes Made Me Do It! A Scientific Look at Sexual Orientation* (Lafayette, La.: Huntington House Publishers, 1999), 209.

20. C. Mann, "Genes and Behavior," *Science* 264 (1994): 1687.

21. Pete Winn, "A Crack in the Wall? A Respected Psychiatrist Rethinks Homosexuality," *CitizenLink: Family Issues in Policy and Culture,* 21 February 2000, <http:www.family.org/cforum/hotissues/a0009548.html>.

Appendix

1. Bennett, "Mixed Blessings."

2. Sacred Congregation for the Doctrine of the Faith, "Declaration on Certain Questions Concerning Sexual Ethics" (Washington, D.C.: United States Catholic Conference, 1977): 106.

3. "Call to Full Humanity," Resolution 1.10; The Lambeth Conference, 1998.

4. "Report of the Baptist Faith and Message Study Committee to the Southern Baptist Convention" (9 June 1998), quoted in Bennett, 10.